SHAREPOINT®
in Practice

Proven methods
to engage your team
& build your company portal

Gerry Brimacombe

SharePoint in Practice: Proven methods to engage your team & build your company portal – Enhanced Version. by Gerry Brimacombe

ISBNs:
Enhanced version – print: 978-1-9995132-3-8
Enhanced version – ebook: 978-1-9995132-0-7
Enhanced version – audio: 978-1-9995132-2-1
Basic version – ebook: 978-1-9995132-1-4

Lightlever Systems Inc.
11055 Finch Place
Ladysmith, BC V9G 1Y9

https://lightlever.ca

Contents

Access to Online Resources

This is the enhanced version of *SharePoint in Practice*. As such, many downloadable templates and working examples are available to you. The login information is below. Please do not share this login information. Once you download the templates, you are free to edit and use them as you wish.

Site: https://lightlever.sharepoint.com/sites/book1

login: reader@sharepointinpractice.com

Password: Pr@ctic@l!

Preface

A N INTRANET PORTAL CAN TRANSFORM THE WAY YOUR COMPANY WORKS. It can empower communication, encourage collaboration, and bring everyone a bit closer. Choosing SharePoint as the platform for that portal is a good choice, especially with the advent of Office 365 and its huge, integrated set of available tools. SharePoint is such a feature-rich and powerful tool, however, that it can be confusing and difficult.

A tool should make a job faster, easier, or better. How can SharePoint be used to build an intranet, a portal, that supports *better communication and collaboration in an organization*? How can you get good—or *GREAT!*—results?

Often, the most straightforward strategy for success is mastering the basics. My dad was a jack-of-all-trades with grade 6 education and limited resources. In the 1970s he decided to move his young family (us) off the grid. He bought a used fishing scow for $1,200, with a plan to build a floating home. He had no money and little experience, but in the winter of 1974 we moved into "the floathouse" and I started some of the best years of my young life.

My dad accomplished this big project with help from friends and mastery of basic tools. We had no electricity, so the work was done with little more than a handsaw, a hammer, and Al Brimacombe's skill with a double-bladed axe.

Similarly, this book describes and demonstrates practical techniques to get good results with the basic SharePoint toolset. You will apply simple, tested, out-of-the-box methods, templates, and examples to build your intranet, or almost any SharePoint business system. This book will save you money and time as you build an intranet that works. If you know your tools, use templates, and involve users, you can get good, fast, and inexpensive results.

Building a SharePoint intranet is like building that float house. We have a platform to start with and a collection of tools and materials that the builder can use to create whatever's needed. With SharePoint we have lists, libraries, wiki pages, and permissions structures that we can pull out-of-the-box.

And, like my dad did with the float house, you will involve your users in the intranet vision and the design so they feel a sense of ownership and are eager to use the end result.

In this book, core concepts will be explained through description and anecdotes, and the companion site, **https://sharepointinpractice.com**, provides real examples and downloadable templates for you to copy and use as you wish.

Please let me know what you think of this book; it and the results it may achieve are a collaboration between myself, my clients, and you.

Gerry Brimacombe
gerry@lightlever.ca

A note about terminology: "intranet" vs. "portal"

So what are we talking about building? We often see the terms "intranet," "portal," "staff portal," and "company portal," so what do we call this thing?

Actually, I usually hear these terms used interchangeably. In the real world, the distinction between "portal" and "intranet" is subtle enough that *SharePoint in Practice* uses both terms equally. (Some argue that "intranet" is the technology and "portal" is the implementation of that technology, but practically speaking, the difference is not significant.)

What you actually build—and what you call it—depends on your needs. What is important is that you can use SharePoint to create a secure system that supports staff and contractors to access and share information from wherever they wish.

PART 1

SharePoint in Practice
Techniques

CHAPTER 1

Introduction to
SharePoint in Practice

S HAREPOINT IN PRACTICE IS A WAY OF THINKING COUPLED WITH A TOOL-
SET THAT LEVERAGES THAT THINKING TO PRODUCE GREAT RESULTS.

The *SharePoint in Practice* Philosophy

The *SharePoint in Practice* philosophy, or way of thinking, underpins all that we do and prints the patterns for how we do it. You will see references to this philosophy throughout the book.

Fundamentally, the *SharePoint in Practice* philosophy is *"TIKI"*:

TEMPLATES: We use and reuse standard templates. By re-using prewritten documents and tested processes we can save time and, even more importantly, improve the quality of our results. Much of this book, and all of the templates included on the website, are copied from actual projects and refined over time. To use that old saw: *No need to reinvent the wheel.*

INVOLVEMENT: We engage and involve end-users and decision makers throughout the project. By engaging a broad spectrum of people, you will get better results and much better buy-in to your new intranet solution.

KISS: We "Keep it Simple SharePoint." We aim to use basic, out-of-the-box SharePoint as much as possible. There are a lot of fancy things that can be done in portal development, and they often bring value, but at what cost? We believe and promote that the simplest solution is usually the best, especially in the first release.

ITERATIONS: We approach our work iteratively. Start rough and collaborate with others to refine over time. This way stakeholders see results faster and can influence development more effectively. And by presenting a work in progress and asking users to help refine it, they feel more like inventors and less like observers.

Use your *SharePoint in Practice* TIKI torch to shine a light on a better portal! (Yes, bad jokes are also part of the tool set.) Applying TIKI is a huge step forward. If you use this philosophy and repeat the TIKI mantra over and over while designing, building, and managing your portal project, you will increase clarity, reduce risk, and greatly increase the value delivered. And everyone will enjoy the process much more.

SharePoint in Practice Templates

Throughout this book, and downloadable from **https://lightlever. sharepoint.com/sites/book1**, you will see over 30 templates ranging from training materials to project plans. These support the "T" in TIKI. By filling in blanks rather than starting with a blank page, you're miles ahead. Of course, templates are not completed documents—they are

---

To access on-line content, log in into the Office 365 companion site. Go to **https://lightlever.sharepoint.com/sites/book1** and login with:

Login: reader@sharepointinpractice.com
Password: Pr@ctic@l!

Please don't share this login information.

a starting point that needs some editing and adapting to your specific situation. Still, this approach is far better than starting from scratch.

See contextual links throughout this book, or review all and download what you need from **https://sharepointinpractice.com/resources/**.

A word about copy/paste and templates.

Control+C and Control+V—the keyboard shortcuts for copying and pasting—are your friends. They save time and reduce errors, just like document templates.

I would much rather start with a template and chop sections out than make up the structure as I go. With the *SharePoint in Practice* templates, the structure has already been set up, which frees you to focus on content.

See a list of templates included with this book in **Appendix A** and on **sharepointinpractice.com/resources**.

CHAPTER 2

Managing Your Portal Project

G OOD PROJECT MANAGEMENT IS ARGUABLY THE MOST IMPORTANT FAC-
TOR IN SUCCESSFULLY BUILDING A COMPANY PORTAL. A well-planned
and well-managed project will save money, reduce stress, and
make everyone look good.

Let's see how we efficiently manage a portal development project.

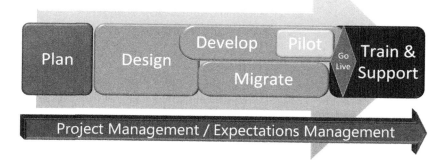

Figure 1 - Portal Development Project Plan Components

Planning

A Project Plan, like any document, is a communication tool. Its primary purpose is to clearly specify what is being done, when and at what cost to achieve the project outcomes, so the project can be managed. Always think of *audience* and *purpose* when writing anything. A key step early in your plan is to present the plan and get sign-off from the Project Sponsor.

Remember the first element of the *SharePoint in Practice* mantra "*TIKI*" is "templates." Start with a Project Plan or Project Charter template, involve stakeholders to create a rough draft, keep it simple, and go back to refine and clarify until everyone agrees and can sign-off.

For smaller projects or those where the Project Sponsor or executive has less interest in detail, you can also use the Project Charter, which pares the plan down to just the basics.

> **TEMPLATE: Portal Development Project Plan**
>
> **TEMPLATE: Project Charter**
>
> **Purpose:** To capture, communicate and approve the scope, cost, schedule and other details of the project.
>
> **Audience:** Project Sponsor, Steering Committee, Project Manager.
>
> Download templates at **https://lightlever.sharepoint.com/sites/book1**

Creating a Project Plan that is both *thorough* and *simple* is a tricky balance. To stay focused on that balance, consistently refer to the *Project Management Iron Triangle*. This pragmatic model has been covered extensively in project management literature, so here I'll just remind you that the three main constraints on a project are time, money, and scope. (*Scope* here means the quantity and quality of work.)

The crux of it is, your project management decisions result in trade-offs between these three constraints.

For example:

- *add more work* and the project will *take longer* or *cost more* (↑scope = ↑time and/or ↑cost);

- *shorten the timeline* and you need to either add more developers and/or use off-the-shelf products, or *reduce how much* you plan to accomplish (↓time = ↑cost and/or ↓scope);

- *a reduced budget* mean you must *do less* or *take longer*, fitting the work in when you can or using lower cost, less skilled people (↓cost = ↓scope and/or ↑time).

In simple terms, ask the Steering Committee, early and frequently, "Do you want the portal good, fast or cheap? Pick any two!" Capture their choice in the Project Plan and manage accordingly.

Project Sponsor and Steering Committee

Your company portal touches all aspects of your organization, so be sure to involve the broadest possible set of executive sponsors. First, formally recognize and name a **Project Sponsor.** This is the manager or executive in the organization who represents the project amongst their peers to approve budgets, manage scope, and address issues. The Sponsor is your ally and your champion, supporting project execution and keeping you honest.

To create an efficient decision-making process in your project, form a **Project Steering Committee**. This group includes representatives from all the key divisions of the company, especially IT, HR, Communications, and Finance.

TEMPLATE: Steering Committee Terms of Reference

Purpose: Identify and communicate the structure and purpose of the Portal Development Steering Committee.

Audience: Project Sponsor, Steering Committee

Download templates at **https://lightlever.sharepoint. com/sites/book1**

Usually, the Steering Committee meets monthly and is chaired by the Project Sponsor. The actual task of running the meetings may fall on the shoulders of the Project Manager (you), and that is fine if the Sponsor has delegated that responsibility to you. Just make sure to keep meetings crisp, and don't waste this group's time.

The Steering Committee receives and reviews project status reports and change requests and is invited to provide feedback and direction on all key project decisions.

Remember that these people are just people, and they want to look good and feel good. Good project results are the best way to make the Steering Committee shine in the eyes of the corporation. Don't waste their time but be prepared to (conscientiously) call or email a Steering Committee member between meetings if you need a quick decision or word of support.

Document Sign-Off

Getting approval signatures, or "sign-off," of project milestones and documents is very important. Key agreements must be recorded so all project participants are able to look back at *what was agreed when* without relying only on memory. So, when the Project Plan (change request, the Design Document, etc.) is reviewed and approved, make sure to get a signature from the Project Sponsor and any other key stakeholders.

TEMPLATE: Steering Committee Kick-Off Presentation

Document Purpose: Provide project overview to the Project Development Steering Committee.

Audience: Project Sponsor, Steering Committee

Download templates at
https://lightlever.sharepoint. com/sites/book1

TEMPLATE: Sign-Off Sheet

Purpose: to capture approval or document completion of a key project artifact or phase. This page is often embedded in a key document or can also be used stand-alone.

Audience: Project Sponsor, Steering Committee

Download templates at
https://lightlever.sharepoint. com/sites/book1

Documenting a milestone is not the most important reason to get ink on paper, however. People will read a document more carefully when they know they will need to sign it later, so sign-off is in part an attention-getting technique. Make sure it's clear—in the project plan and via face-to-face and email communications (yes, you will repeat yourself)—that these documents will need formal sign-off.

As for obtaining sign-off, sometimes hunting down an executive with a signature page in your hand is the best way. However, if you don't need a wet signature for legal or policy reasons, you can employ the simpler approach of emailing the executive with a message: "*Please reply to this email to indicate approval of the attached.*" Then screen capture and paste their email response onto the signature page of the document for filing.

As mentioned above, obtaining sign-off is crucial, so even though it can be a hassle, don't get lazy on this one. (Rest assured that many other opportunities to be lazy are included elsewhere in this book.)

Managing Expectations

As Stephen Covey teaches, you must "begin with the end in mind."[1] You've clearly documented project goals and what needs to be done, by when, and how much it will cost. You have a plan that all have agreed upon and you're done, right? Not so fast! It's time to talk about expectations.

Throughout the project, you must constantly manage people's expectations. In a design meeting, someone may excitedly ask, "*Can we also make the font larger for announcement titles?*" or an executive will suggest, "*Everyone is very busy, so can we just skip the next meeting?*" Your answer is always along the lines of "*Yes, but there's a tradeoff.*" Remember the Project Management Iron Triangle above? Stay positive and encouraging of everyone's ideas—you want people to be creative—but always manage your budget, scope, and timeline. This means managing expectations.

---

1   Covey, Stephen R. *The 7 Habits of Highly Effective People: Restoring the Character Ethic.* [Rev. ed.]. New York: Free Press, 2004.

You will often hear consultants say, "under-promise and over-deliver," which is another way of looking at expectation management. If you paint a picture that is too rosy—too optimistic—you may find yourself in trouble when things don't go exactly as planned. By constantly, and sometimes subtly, managing the expectations of the Project Sponsor, the Steering Committee, the Design Team and others, you are keeping everyone on side with what _we can realistically accomplish_. (Yes, the "we" is emphasized—when done well, expectations management helps create a stronger team culture as _we_ work together to overcome the constraints of time, budget, and schedule.

So, what do I mean by "expectations management"? We're talking about setting appropriate expectation all project team members and the executive—what can be delivered, by when.

First, don't just take the easy route of the pessimist and paint a picture of doom and gloom—the project team wants to hear that we can and will succeed. Do, however, stay realistic and cautious. Resist the temptation to say "yes" to everyone's great ideas. Keep the Iron Triangle in mind always. Refer to the Project Plan and use your knowledge of SharePoint to manage change. Change always affects the project triple-constraints. Explain how resources (time and money) are finite, and so we need to proceed judiciously. If we try to do too much, no one wins.

SharePoint in Practice philosophy TIKI point #3—"Keep it Simple SharePoint"—is important in terms of handling expectations. This rule says we use out-of-the-box SharePoint as much as is practical. If you have enough development budget and time, consider including those features that may require (for example) SharePoint Workflow or JavaScript. Just be careful of scope creep.

Explain to your enthusiastic design team that out-of-the-box SharePoint solutions are easier to build and maintain by a factor of 10 or so, and when it comes time to upgrade SharePoint to a newer version, that install could well be complicated by any non-standard development work in place. Help them to choose. If it's decided that _yes_, this change is worth the effort, then use the formal change request process described below to document the decision and get approval from the Project Sponsor.

Status Reporting

One of the most effective habits of a well-run project is reliable project status reporting. When planning your project, plan to produce weekly or bi-weekly status reports to distribute to the Steering Committee and other interested stakeholders. The status report is a short (1-2 page) format that quickly and colorfully shows the pulse of the project: what we are working on, what we need to resolve, and the current state of schedule and budget.

The status report lets everyone know what's up with the project, but there's more! I have discovered over the years that a big added value of regular status reporting is to remind *me* (the Project Manager) of next steps and keep *me* cognizant of budget and schedule. Use your routine project status report as a regularly scheduled *drumbeat of accountability* that keeps you and everyone else on track and aligned with what was agreed in the Project Plan.

> **TEMPLATE:** Project Status Report
>
> **Document Purpose:** Communicate project progress and issues; help the PM stay on task.
>
> **Audience:** Project Sponsor, Steering Committee, Project Manager, Project Team members
>
> Download templates at **https://lightlever.sharepoint.com/sites/book1**

Change Management

Change is inevitable. When writing the Project Plan, we do our best to foresee what will happen and how the project will go, but that is never entirely accurate. Embrace this fact. Accepting the imperfection of your ability to see exactly what's coming frees you up to develop a project plan that is not stuck in the paralysis of analysis. Include change control as part of the plan from the outset so you can move forward efficiently.

> **TEMPLATE:** Project Change Request
>
> **Document Purpose:** Analyze and communicate any change to scope, timeline, budget, or project approach.
>
> **Audience:** Project Sponsor, Project Steering Committee
>
> Download templates at **https://lightlever.sharepoint.com/sites/book1**

Set expectations and train the Steering Committee and the Project Sponsor that any change in the project, even if it is just a clarification and even if it doesn't affect budget or schedule, will be documented with a formal change request process. Here again, attitude is important. The change request is planned and presented as a *communication tool*. A well-written change request helps the Project Manager quantify and clarify the impacts of every change. It also uses a standard structure that summarizes the impacts, so the Sponsor and Steering Committee *can understand* the change and make good decisions. Asking for sign-off of every change keeps the responsibility for project decisions where it belongs—with the Project Sponsor supported by the Steering Committee.

Go-Live Planning

The milestone when the new portal is complete and available to all users is called "Go-Live," "Launch," or the "cutover date." This is a key milestone, obviously, with a lot going on.

Referring to the Go-Live Plan template, you will see communication, technical, and training tasks connected to this event.

If possible, schedule your Go-Live date to be a Monday, so you can work on final steps over the weekend, especially final migration and menus. The Monday timing also imparts a "fresh start" feeling, which can be very effective. When your organization doesn't have down time—for example, the operation is open all weekend—you may need to organize and communicate some "gray area" time, when the new portal will be in the process of being implemented and old systems might still be available.

> **TEMPLATE:** Go-Live Plan
>
> **Purpose:** To lay out in detail all tasks to support a smooth implementation. To draft communications so they are ready to go when necessary.
>
> **Audience:** Steering Committee, Migration Team, Development Team, all staff
>
> Download templates at **https://lightlever.sharepoint.com/sites/book1**

Go-Live Communications

Well-timed communications are designed to keep stakeholders and the broader user base informed of what's going on and when. There are few things people like less than a surprise when they are trying to work. You will find communications templates in the above-referenced Go-Live Plan. Note the attempt to be clear yet brief. This is challenging, so each communique starts with a brief sentence or paragraph that summarizes the critical information, and then proceeds to details, usually bulleted. You will also note that our Portal Purpose Statement is frequently reiterated (more about that in **Chapter 3** (page 17)).

The Technical Tricks of Go-Live

The technical side of launching the company portal can be complicated. This process must be carefully planned and managed to minimize disruption and corporate confusion. Again, refer to the Go-Live Plan template and consider:

Migration: Is content completely migrated? Has metadata been set? Has a search *full crawl* run since content migration completed, so that the new content is searchable? If wiki pages were migrated, have all links been updated to point to the new site content?

Theme: It is easy to change the SharePoint theme (colors, font, and Oslo vs Seattle layout). What makes this easy, of course, is our *SharePoint in Practice* KISS mentality, and therefore the use of standard templates without much programming involved. One potential challenge is changing from a Seattle theme, which has a Quick Launch on the left and a top menu, to Oslo style, which (strangely) eliminates the top menu and moves the left nav to the top of the page.

Home Page: If you are building a site where the address remains the same—building *in situ*—then you can build the new home page during the development phase, and just before launch, use the Wiki Page command "Set as Home Page" to replace the old page with new.

If you will be using a new web address, you will need to involve the technical or IT team to switch DNS settings. This process can take up to 48 hours, so plan ahead.

Menus: When developing a SharePoint portal on top of an existing site, the switch to a new home page is simple. Not so with menus. As soon as you start to create a new top menu or the Quick Launch (left nav) menu, you run the risk of changing the behavior of the existing site before you or the users are ready. Consider the impacts carefully. You may find it best to build the menu in Managed Metadata in advance and deploy at the last minute, or you may just have all your menus and links in a file suitable for copy-paste and build the menus as part of the Go-Live activities.

Training: You have been training your development team and executives throughout the project, and now is the time to get the rest of the company up to speed. If you expect to have a company portal that is heavily used by a broad user base for advanced document management and intense collaboration, plan some significant training. If, on the other hand, this will be a system where most people need minimal training, a Go-Live Webinar will be enough. This webinar is offered to all staff. See **Go-Live Webinar** in **Chapter 9** (page 97) for more details.

Go-Live Contest: An effective training and engagement method is to develop a SharePoint Survey in a contest format. This "go-live contest" encourages users to walk through the new portal and develop basic skills training. This contest is mentioned here for completeness, and details can be found in **Go-Live Contest** in **Chapter 6** (page 61).

CHAPTER 3

Designing Your Portal

W ITH A GOOD PROJECT MANAGEMENT STRUCTURE IN PLACE, IT IS TIME TO DISCUSS AND DOCUMENT YOUR PORTAL DESIGN. Engaging and educating key users is an important byproduct of this process.

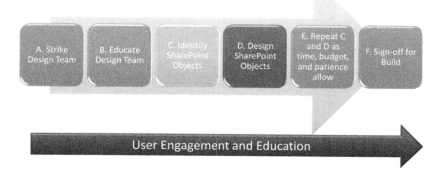

Figure 2 - User Engagement and Education

The keystone document for this phase, and for the rest of the project, is the **Design Document**, which acts as a discussion platform now, and a constant reference during the build. You will use this design phase to define the portal and systematically engage and educate the users. In the Development Phase, you will further refine and enhance the design through live demonstration.

The Design Team

People support what they create. Bring together a group to determine what the portal should include, how it should work, and who can do what.

The **Design Team** is, of course, a *committee*. An effective committee has a clear mandate, is well-organized and carefully facilitated. To accomplish this, use a simple Terms of Reference document, approved by the Project Manager and the Project Sponsor or executive team.

> **TEMPLATE:** Design Team Terms of Reference
>
> **Purpose:** To clarify, communicate, and agree upon the roles and responsibilities of the Design Team.
>
> **Audience:** Steering Committee, Design Team
>
> Download templates at **https://lightlever.sharepoint. com/sites/book1**

Armed with your Terms of Reference, recruit the team.

Create a Design Team with as much variety as possible. You won't achieve perfection, but try to get managers and staff from *all business areas*— especially Communications, IT, HR, Finance, and the Executive. This cross-section of business areas creates a dynamic group with a variety of perspectives. People are often energized by working with colleagues they rarely meet, and an energetic group is more fun, creative, and productive.

It is vital to include the *front-line staff*—the people who understand the daily challenges and know what is needed to support the business of the organization. They have the motivation and the ideas to design a portal that will support a create business operation.

You may question the value of "design by committee," but this is a powerful process when the committee is run well. With teamwork and leadership, your committee will synergize to produce great ideas and a sense of accomplishment. And they will come to understand the portal deeply through that process.

Now let's get that team busy!

The Design Process

You will lead meetings with the Design Team on a regular basis. Usually these design meetings are held every two weeks, but you may choose weekly, especially if there is a push to get the project complete fast. In any case, at the beginning of this phase, send Outlook invitations to the team to get all meetings in their calendars and the rooms booked.

To engage your users throughout the project and co-create a system, I want to stress the value of having the right *attitude*. *SharePoint in Practice* is about developing a company portal that people will use. With an attitude of openness and curiosity, *collaborate* to create a *collaborative system*.

In each design meeting, you will come prepared with the Design Document (barely more than a template in the first meeting) and will conduct the meeting based on the following agenda (to be included in the meeting invitations). Note that the agenda may vary from meeting to meeting—for example, the first meeting will focus more on the Project Plan, and the last meeting will focus more on Permissions.

Sample Agenda, First Design Meeting

MEETING OBJECTIVES
NOTE: Every meeting should have a clearly stated purpose or objectives.

1. Ensure shared understanding of the Project Plan;
2. Brainstorm business challenges to be solved by the portal project;
3. Work to define the purpose of the new portal;
4. Brainstorming-style discussion to start portal design.

AGENDA
1. **Project overview (10 minutes)**
   NOTE: Refer to your project plan extensively.

2. **Define Portal Purpose Statement (10 minutes)**
   NOTE: Use a straw dog approach, based on the draft supplied below.

3. **Demonstrate sample intranet portals (15 minutes)**
   NOTE: Demonstrate portals you have built or have access to, or contact Gerry to do this piece for you.

4. **Brainstorm key objects and structure (20 minutes)**
   NOTE: Keep this light and fast-moving to capture a quantity of ideas over quality. Don't judge the ideas or get into too much detail; just let them flow.

> **TEMPLATE:** Design Team Kick-off Presentation
>
> **Purpose:** To get the team clear on what they are to do, and how, and working in the same direction
>
> **Audience:** Design Team
>
> Download templates at **https://lightlever.sharepoint.com/sites/book1**

5. **Discuss design guidelines (10 minutes)**
   NOTE: Draft design guidelines are in the Design Document template below.

6. **Next steps (5 minutes)**
   NOTE: What do we have coming up? The next Design Meeting, for sure. What about actions or activities? Reiterate them here.

Sample Agenda, Subsequent Design Meetings

MEETING OBJECTIVES

1. Convey any changes to the Project Plan;

2. Continue discussion to design the new portal;

3. Raise issues and concerns and work them through.

AGENDA

1. **Review agenda (5 minutes)**
   NOTE: This gives you an opportunity to review what will be discussed, and how. Since this is a standard agenda, this will be brief, but we allocate 5 minutes to buy some time in case people arrive late.

2. **Review information architecture draft to date (15 minutes)**

NOTE: If you are working on the IA, this should be presented and discussed. This may be part of the Design Document.

3. **Review changes to design (35 minutes)**
   NOTE: This is the bulk of the meeting. You will have the Design Document projected at the front of the room with changes since last meeting tracked. Invite discussion and provide ad hoc training.

4. **Next steps (5 minutes)**
   NOTE: What do we have coming up? The next Design Meeting? What about actions or activities? Reiterate them here.

Portal Purpose Statement

The first task for the newly formed Design Team is to state the purpose of the corporate portal.

What business problems are we trying to solve? These may already be stated and available as part of a project definition, project charter, or employee satisfaction survey. If not, define them with your team now. These problem statements will feed into the purpose statement used in design, development, project management, and key communications.

Here are some examples of business problems to be solved:

- Staff struggle with and are frustrated by current systems.

- Staff can't find the information they need to do their jobs.

- Company appears old-fashioned or unprofessional because the portal is outdated or nonexistent.

> **EXAMPLE**
>
> **Portal Purpose Statement:**
>
> <Our portal> helps staff communicate, collaborate, and manage information to support each other and better serve our customers.
>
> OR
>
> <our intranet> helps all staff quickly find the information they need to support the strategic work of the organization.

- Staff waste time recreating information rather than finding what has already been created and re-using it.

- Old technology no longer serves users' needs.

- Old technology is no longer supported by the vendor.

- People in different branches are working well together and may not even know each other.

Straw Dog Iteration

As per the TIKI guideline #2, *Iterate*, the best way to support and utilize the Design Team is using a *straw dog* (or *straw man*) approach: Initially, build something quick and rough, and then allow people to criticize and question your draft before a lot of effort has been expended. And rather than starting with a blank whiteboard, the straw dog gives them a starting point and a better sense of the goal. This approach has been labeled *pretotyping*[2], and it can be a very powerful technique.

For example, we apply the straw dog approach to develop the Portal Purpose Statement. It's easy to waste valuable time with 10 people "wordsmithing." To shortcut that process, create an initial statement that people can examine, judge, and question. This will create a huge step toward agreement. Start with a statement like the one drafted in the box above, tweak it to fit your needs, and present it for people to criticize and build upon.

Sometimes an initial statement is embraced and finalized very quickly, and at other times, much time and effort are spent refining the exact wording. In the latter situation, when you seem to be "writing by committee" and the energy in the room starts to drag, then table it, saying, *"Please think about this, and we'll revisit it when we meet again in two weeks. In the meantime, feel free to email me with any ideas or thoughts you may have."*

> **Occam's razor:** Given multiple solutions to a problem, we should always choose the simplest solution.

---

2   **http://www.pretotyping.org/** "MAKE SURE YOU ARE BUILDING *THE RIGHT* IT BEFORE YOU BUILD *IT* RIGHT."

The Design Document

The Design Document is a living document that captures all high-level details of what you will build. This critical, keystone document is used and updated throughout the entire *SharePoint in Practice* process, including design, development, training, governance, and maintenance.

The Design Document fulfills the following functions:

- captures and shares design decisions (what is to be built);

- captures and communicates SharePoint permissions guidelines and structure;

- drives and supports the portal build phase;

- captures ideas for the future to minimize discussion time in meetings;

- provides a foundation for training materials;

- provides a foundation for governance materials; and

- acts as system documentation to support knowledge transfer, troubleshooting, and future development.

TEMPLATE: Portal Design Document

Purpose: To capture and communicate all decisions about how the portal will look and act. This includes structure, objects, metadata, and permissions. Also used as a reference for training and site maintenance.

Audience: Design Team, all Stakeholders, Developers.

Download templates at **https://lightlever.sharepoint.com/sites/book1**

Like almost everything in *SharePoint in Practice*, the Design Document starts with a template. Let's walk through that template.

Section 1 – Introduction

This section introduces the document and the portal design. It provides an overview of the project and includes the purpose statement mentioned above. This sets the context of why you are building this company portal and what are you trying to accomplish.

Depending on your organization and if you feel it is important, a background section, history, or business drivers may also be included here.

Section 2 – Structure

This section describes the overall structure and context, including an image depicting the overview of the planned site. It also includes a description of the main site menu; color choices; whether the layout will be Oslo, Seattle, or customized; screen layouts; and any font choices or other design guidelines. In short, this section should include anything that affects the entire site or site collection.

Site Structure Diagram

The structural overview diagram is very useful and widely applied. This schematic visually represents what is to be built and how it is structured.

The shapes and colors here break up the monotony of a straight text design document and improve your odds of catching the Design Team's attention (and thereby better engaging them to participate fully). This diagram is also used to plan permissions inheritance and may be repurposed as an image on the site to allow all users to see a structural overview or even to navigate the site.

TEMPLATE: Portal Design Graphics

Purpose: Graphical tool to draw and communicate portal structure and page layout wire frames.

Audience: Design Team, Developers, all staff

Download templates at
https://lightlever.sharepoint. com/sites/book1

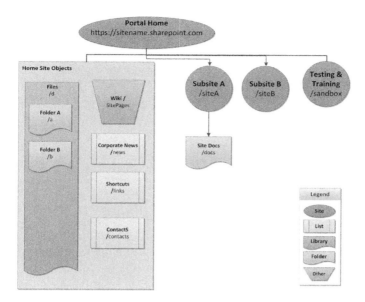

Figure 3 - Sample Portal Structure Diagram

I recommend Visio to produce this diagram, though you could also use SmartArt or PowerPoint for a very simple site. Copy and paste as an image into the Word document. (Embedded Visio can be problematic and not worth the trouble, so *paste special* as "*Picture (enhanced metafile)*").

Especially for visually oriented people, this diagram provides a better understanding of the planned portal and as a result, a deeper sense of connection. Of course, creating this diagram takes additional work—as objects are added, removed, or renamed, the image must also be updated—but it is worthwhile work.

Note with the example provided above, the relative URLs of all the SharePoint objects are included. This is optional but adds clarity and is especially useful if you plan to reuse the image as a navigation tool.

Section 3 – Object Details

The third section of the Design Document is the object details section. Each object in the site—key pages, lists, libraries, and subsites—has a subsection. The content in this section will be copy/pasted extensively during the development phase, so keep that in mind while writing. Again, think of your audience, which in this case includes SharePoint list names and descriptions, field names and descriptions, choice fields, etc. that will be pasted into SharePoint and consumed by all portal users.

This section provides the bulk of the design. Describe everything you are going to build at the level of detail suitable to build it in SharePoint.

EXAMPLE

Here's a sample entry from the design document *Object Details* section, with [*Notes*].

3.14 Useful Links

[*The title of this sub-section is also copy/pasted to create the "friendly name" of the SharePoint object.*]

Web Address: /links [*This is the short name copy/pasted to initially create the list and so becomes part of the URL.*]
SharePoint Description: *Shortcuts and web links relevant to all staff and targetable to specif departments.* [*The SharePoint Description will be pasted into the Description field when creating the object.*]

[*What follows is a general, descriptive text for the Design Team. May include behavior, permissions notes, metadata or global content references, etc. May be used in Governance Guide.*]

This is a standard List of Links. This is used to provide shortcuts to external and internal sites and files.

[*The following table defines custom fields and will be used when building list and libraries.*]

Metadata Field	Data Type	Mandatory?	Default	Description
[Users see field names in list views and when adding, editing, or viewing list items. Will be copy/pasted when creating fields.]	[In some cases copy/ pasted, e.g. for Choice fields.]	[Is the user required to enter this field? Setting for "Require that this column contains information:".]	[Copy/ paste as field default value.]	[Will be visible to users on standard New and Edit forms. Copy/paste into field description.]
Target Audience	Managed Metadata "Department"	No	Blank	Which department needs to see this link? If blank, then it means "all departments" and is shown on home page
Importance	Choice: 1-Low 2-Medium 3-HIGH	No	2-Medium	How important is this link? Consider how often will it be used and by how many people.
Sequence	Number	No	50	Sequence number to sort the links

Views

[The list or library views that will be created for this object. First the name, which will be copy/pasted and users will see (and need to understand), followed by a brief description for developers on how the view is to be structured.]

1. *All Links:* all links default view, showing metadata

2. *Home Page View:* showing links URL only, non-tabular view, sorted by *Seq* and filtering so only items where *Target Audience* is blank.

3. *Department Page View:* showing links URL only, non-tabular view, sorted by *Seq* and filtering so only items where *Target Audience* is <department name>; will be created as a stub and added/edited on department wiki pages.

It is important to note that the Design Document is a high-level document. (As a friend of mine used to say, *"We don't want to program in Word. Let's get that part over with so we can do the fun stuff."*) Keep document writing effort to a minimum so that you can focus the energy, resources, and real work on developing with SharePoint. And, of course, the larger any document gets, the less likely anyone will read and understand it. Use simple, results-focused statements and descriptions in the Design Document, such as, *"This is a standard announcements list with the following modifications..."* Stay practical!

Critical to design process and meetings, and a key tenet to the *SharePoint in Practice* philosophy, is to ensure that you are involving team members while managing expectations. We recommend using SharePoint out-of-the-box tools and educating the team about these tools as you go. You want to listen to all ideas, and sometimes it is necessary to address an idea by explaining that with your timeline and budget you don't have the capability to develop an advanced feature. This was discussed in **Managing Expectations** in **Chapter 2** (page 11).

Section 4 – Global Content

Global content describes any objects that are used throughout the site or site collection, not specific to one page or list or library. This includes the information architecture or taxonomy of the site, site columns, content types, and workflows.

Section 5 – Search

Search is a critical success factor for a company portal. From a *SharePoint in Practice* point of view, where we use out-of-the-box tools as much as possible, search customizations are minimal: adding search refiners and updating to result sources are usually sufficient. This section describes what is to be done with the search page as well as any other design decisions that affect search, such as metadata and file naming conventions.

Section 6 – Permissions Plan

This section is a detailed breakdown of permissions or access rights for the portal. It is structured to be understandable, implementable, and maintainable. We start by acknowledging that SharePoint permissions are complex. Take care with your permissions design or you may have a permissions structure that is difficult to build and maintain. And of course, permissions that are not implemented correctly can cause embarrassment and even liability in the organization if people see what they should not be allowed to see.

We design and implement permissions via manageable steps in order to simplify the process and better understand and communicate each facet of this complex structure. Here is the overview, which starts here in the Design Phase and continues into development:

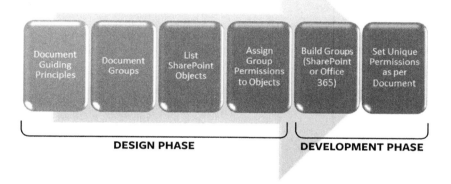

Figure 4 - Permissions Implementation Process

Guiding Principles

The first subsection of the permissions plan is *guiding principles*. Again, if you are starting with the Design Document template, you already have much of this in hand and can edit to suit your needs. Try to create rules that meet the corporate needs while remaining understandable and implementable.

EXAMPLE

Permissions Guiding Principles

1. Unless required to be locked down for privacy or security, permissions will be open (read, write, edit, delete) for all staff.

2. Permissions for a department are managed by that department's Content Steward(s) and the SharePoint Administrators.

3. For Site Pages (wiki pages), all users can edit pages owned by their department, and all staff can read all pages.

4. Permissions should always be set by Group rather than by individual.

5. Wherever possible, Groups will reflect departments, teams, committees, or other corporate roles.

6. The SharePoint Access Request feature will be turned off.

A key permissions principle worth discussing here is *"Unless required to be locked down for privacy or security, permissions will be open to all staff."* In other words, as much as possible, everyone can read/write everything on the company portal.

This "open by default" rule simplifies the design, development, implementation, and maintenance of your site. This principle will require discussion and explanation, as most people want to apply all sorts of complex permissions to make sure other people don't *mess with their stuff*. Work to distinguish the fear from the true need. Explain that we already trust each other (and have employment agreements in place) to keep corporate information safe and secure without overburdening our business processes with complex system controls. And explain that a company portal works best when we view the content as "our files" rather than "my files." The content belongs to the organization, and the organization trusts its staff to handle materials appropriately. The more we can trust each other, the more useful the portal becomes.

Remember this is *SharePoint in Practice,* and one of the guiding principles is *KISS,* or Keep it Simple SharePoint. By designing permissions structures that are *simpler,* you're designing a portal this is easier to build, easier to understand, and easier to maintain. Explain these concepts to the Design Team and respect their knowledge of the business needs. Ultimately you may need to accept their requirement to lock down certain areas or create read-only or "contribute without delete" permissions levels, just make sure they understand the ramifications.

Groups Standards and Listing

Next, list the permission groups. These may be SharePoint groups, Active Directory, or one of the Office 365 security group types. Because we manage permissions by group name, it is important to implement a standard group naming convention that is scalable and that everyone can understand.

This is where the *step-by-step* approach really shines. Rather than trying to wrap our heads around complex permissions and rules about *who can access what and with which permission levels,* we start at the start. The first step defines the user community as logical groups that are usually already well understood by the organization. These groups usually correspond to departments or teams within the business (for example, the Executive Team or the SharePoint Administrators). We include a description of each group in this section and, if wanted for clarity or future copy-and-paste, a listing of the users in each group.

Who Can Do What to What Table

The largest subsection in the permissions plan is the table showing *who can do what to what.* This is arguably the most important section in the entire Design Document.

Securable object (site, list, library, folder, document, or item)	Description	Unique or inherited permissions?	Groups that need permissions	Permission level to assign (Read-only, Contribute, Full Control)
Finance Subsite	The special site for the Finance Department	Unique	Group Name	Permissions
			All Staff	Read
			Finance Staff	Contribute
			SharePoint Admins	Full Control

Figure 5 - Example Permission Item for Finance Department

Here we list all SharePoint objects in our site, then fill in the blanks: *Will this object inherit permissions from its parent?* (*Great!*) *Or does it require unique permissions?* (*Too bad.*) The objects needing unique permissions are flagged as such and a nested table describes which group has which permission level. Of course, in SharePoint, if we don't give someone access to an object, then people have no access (not even read). Therefore, you only need to list the groups who *do* need permissions to (at least) *Read* the object. That said, for clarity you can add a line to explicitly state *no permissions* for certain groups. For example, you could show the *All Staff* group explicitly as having *no access* to *Board Minutes*, so the Design Team is perfectly clear that everyone is excluded from that library (or folder or list or site). Note that if we follow guiding principle #1, the *All Staff* group will have *Contribute* access to most objects.

Standard and custom permission levels can be referenced here. The most commonly used permission levels are *full control, contribute,* and *read* (read only). You may also include custom permission levels. For example, my clients often ask for a *Contribute without Delete* permission level, so they can specify some groups who can add and edit content but can't delete it.

As with the entire Design Document, the permissions plan is a vehicle for communication. Work through it with your Design Team in the order it is written and discuss and confirm all details in an iterative manner. It's easy for people to get overwhelmed in this section of the design—permissions can be difficult to comprehend—so it is important that you don't rush and don't push too hard. Remember the straw dog (iterative) approach. Create an early draft of the permissions plan, a kind of *permissions plan lite,* and present it to the Design Team with the purpose of explaining the structure and meaning of the tables, and introducing the guiding principles and the thinking behind them. At first, focus less on content and mostly on process and structure: the *how* with a little *what.* Then support the committee to brainstorm and discuss. If the discussion is not productive—you feel you are going around in circles and people don't really understand or they just need more time—then pull back and say, "*Great, good discussion. Permissions are a difficult topic, and we don't have to finish this right now. I'll do some updates based on what I am hearing, and we'll discuss more next time.*"

Respectfully let them off the hook and make full use of your planned iterative approach.

Remember, the permissions plan is a very powerful and important section that will greatly aid you when it comes to implementation, and it will support the SharePoint Admins in doing maintenance and future enhancements.

Section 7 – *Ideas for Future Development*

In practice, we endeavor to keep the design discussion moving forward in a productive and cost-effective development process, so you cannot get deep into the details of everything that comes up. The Design Team can get very creative. It can be tricky to encourage and support that creativity while spending most of your time on what is most important and getting results.

So, we create a "parking lot" for ideas.

As discussed in the chapter on Project Management, your project is limited by time and budget. Any idea that comes up is potential "scope creep." Nobody wins when there is scope creep, so honor the ideas from the team and capture them for future reference rather than including them in the current scope. For example, a team member might suggest a need for a Shopping Cart, where staff can order materials from the head office. If that is within scope, great, include it in Section 3. Give it some design attention and carry on. However, if this a new idea that will stretch the scope of the project, is overly complex, or is not going to fit in the project for whatever reason, then park it in this "Future Development" category. Say, *"Thank you for that suggestion. We'll capture it here for future development and come back to it if we have time or if there is additional budget, such as in a phase 2."*

It is important to capture all ideas for future development and include as much or as little detail as time allows. This section is somewhat free format: some sections are just placeholders, and others may have more detail. Of course, if important details are mentioned, capture them. If somebody adds *"and it has to link to our invoicing system,"* take the 15 seconds to write a bullet that captures that comment.

Just as you approach design iteratively, also recognize and embrace that you are building a foundation upon which future development can and should occur: You will start simply and grow the portal features and functions over time.

Appendices

Last are the appendices, if required. Appendices include information that is not central to the document—for example, a photograph of a whiteboard after a brainstorm session or a card sort from the information architecture.

Design Document Approval

At the end of this phase, you will have a completed Design Document that the Project Sponsor can approve to "go ahead and build based on what's written here." (See **Signing Key Documents** in **Chapter 2** (page 10)). Remember that the Design Document will continue to be updated throughout the rest of the project, so the approval here is not to imply or state that "*This is exactly what will be built, and it won't change*" but rather "*This is accurate and complete at this point. Please sign off so we can move forward.*"

CHAPTER 4

Building Your Portal

YOU NOW HAVE A SIGNED DESIGN DOCUMENT AND CAN PROCEED WITH CONFIDENCE TO BRING THAT DESIGN TO LIFE.

The development phase continues to use the *SharePoint in Practice* interactive, iterative approach. You will refer to the Design Document to build components of the portal and demonstrate and refine them via regular presentations and conversations with the Design Team.

(Note that we assume you are working with an existing SharePoint environment (e.g. Office 365 or SherWeb), and you don't need to purchase SharePoint or configure a server.)

Laying the Ground Work

The development phase doesn't feel very different from the design phase. The key difference is that you will now be showing and updating the new portal live in SharePoint, not just creating and sharing a design document.

Continue to use the Design Team formed earlier for this process. If you need to adjust membership, that's okay, but ask any new members to come up to speed by reading the Design Document. Based on the

Project Plan, schedule all Development Review Meetings. Get these in the calendar to book people and rooms well in advance, and lay down milestones for your development work.

Development is a fun part of the process. This is where users get to see everything they've been discussing and designing come to life. It's like you have been preparing for a big trip: choosing dates and companions, deciding what to bring, getting the right gear, and deciding how to carry it. Now it's all planned, chosen, purchased, and packed, and you finally can enjoy the trip. The fun part. Part of what makes this fun, like any good trip, is good preparation—which is exactly what you have been doing in building relationships, making good plans, and collaborating to create an excellent design.

Be sure to maintain the strong "we are building this together" energy you established during the Design Phase. With this in mind, make sure the portal site under construction is available to the Design Team to test and peruse between meetings, and encourage them to "play with it" as much as they like.

A Few Words About "Development"

In talking about SharePoint development, recognize that our *Share-Point in Practice* KISS approach is "small d" development—sometimes called SharePoint *out-of-the-box*. In computer science, "Development" means coding complex systems with programming languages, test plans, source code management, *and lions and tigers and bears, oh my*! In the *SharePoint in Practice* paradigm, "development" is mostly developing business requirements (the Design Document), and implementing those requirements using the SharePoint web-based interface. Compared to your average system development project, our work with SharePoint is pretty straightforward.

If possible, develop directly in the live SharePoint site. This way the site you are building doesn't need to be migrated or promoted to production. It is live and ready to go at any time. There are ways to adjust that approach to have a test environment or a development site, but unlike a lot of traditional programming, it's a bit more difficult to have those separate environments. You may have a situation where it is necessary, but we won't be addressing dev/test/prod environments and "promotion to production" in this book. Again, we will do our level best to *Keep it Simple Sharepoint.*

The Iterative Build Process

To build your portal, you will continue to use the *SharePoint in Practice* iterative approach.

There are three parts to each development iteration:

1. **Build SharePoint Objects:** These are described in the Design Document. Start with the structure and the most important or most complex objects.

2. **Present:** Facilitate a Development Review meeting to show and discuss the changes since last meeting. Lead an engaged and curious discussion. Take direction and take notes on ideas and decisions for ongoing refinement.

3. **Refine Design:** During and after Review meetings, update the Design Document with any agreed or proposed refinements. Cycle back to "Build SharePoint Objects" to update the portal-under-development in preparation for the next meeting.

Let's look at the first iteration. In fact, you should have already scheduled these meetings with the Design Team. On a large computer monitor, or dual monitors, open both the Design Document and the SharePoint site to be developed. Tile into two windows, each taking half of the screen: Design Document on the left, SharePoint on the right.[3] (We'll copy from the left and paste to the right—that's the way my brain works.) Then proceed to build the SharePoint site while copying

---

3   I am a big fan of the **Windows 10 Snap Assist** feature to quickly tile your monitor with non-overlapping windows.

from the Design Document. (See how-to video: **https://youtu.be/ dFnV2f34zxs.**)

For example, let's say the Design Document describes an object as follows:

> ## 3.2 *Finance Documents*
>
> **Web Address:** */findocs*
> **SharePoint Description:** *Files owned and managed by the finance department.*
>
> etc.

To build the Finance Documents as specified in the Design Document, first, in SharePoint select "Add an app," "Document Library," and select Advanced Options. From the Design Document, copy the Web Address (*findocs*) and paste into SharePoint in the library name field. Then copy the SharePoint Description (*files owned and managed by...*) and paste into the Description field.

Site contents ‣ New

Name and Description
Type a new name as you want it to appear in headings and links throughout the site. Type descriptive text that will help site visitors use this document library.

Name:
findocs

Description:
Files owned and managed by the finance department.

Notice that we create a list or library with the short name, findocs, and then renamed it? Why not just call it *Finance Documents* right away? This is because a) once we create a list or library, the URL cannot be changed; and b) we are trying to keep our URLs short—if we use *Finance Documents*, SharePoint will convert the space to %20 and create the document library URL of *Finance%20Documents*. So, create libraries and lists with short names without spaces and then *rename* them to something more descriptive.

So now we will change the library name from "findocs" to "Finance Documents." For the new *findocs* library, open "Library Settings" and copy/paste the long name from the Design Document.

If refinements or corrections come up during this process, as they usually do, make changes in the Design Document first, and then in SharePoint.

To be clear, let me say that differently: updates to the Design Document can and often do occur while building the site. For example you may come up with better wording for a field description or realize that you need a different field or an additional view. The goal is to keep the Design Document up to date so that at any given time, including the end of the build phase, the Design Document matches the portal. This is a powerful concept—you are building your system documentation as a byproduct of designing and building the intranet.

Proceed to build the objects in the Design Document, copying and pasting wherever you can. There is no spellcheck in most parts of SharePoint development, so it's faster, and more practical, to copy spell-checked text from Word and paste into SharePoint. This helps you avoid the extra work of going back to correct typos, such as having mistyped "field" as "feild."

Prioritize the build. Focus first on the lists or sites that will require the most discussion with the Design Team. For example, one client needed extensive customization on an announcements list. The list was called *Staff Communications*, and the Design Team had come up with several interesting features to manage and use this list. Early in the development, we created the announcements list, customized it, and named it *Staff Communications*. There were several design meetings remaining where I was able to demonstrate the list live, and refine the behavior.

Note that you will build everything with "inherited permissions" at this time. Unique permissions will be applied near the end of the Design Phase.

All this development leads up to the *Present* step of the iteration, where you will show the Design Team what has been developed and changed since the last meeting and ask for their feedback and discussion.

Iteration Timing and Number

Depending on how much time you have as a developer (or a team of developers), the complexity of the site design, and the availability of the Design Team, you may have iterations between one and four weeks in length. Two weeks is usually the sweet spot. This provides a good rhythm, with enough time to build SharePoint objects between meetings and to give people time to digest and adapt or adjust to the changes, without leaving so much of a gap that they forget what was discussed.

Plan all iterations in advance, and book the Design Review meetings (with Outlook calendar invites). These milestones keep you and the team on track. Schedule as many iterations as time and budget allow—usually three or four. If you have designed a complex system, more iterations provide the opportunity for more complex discussion and refinement of the portal.

Development Review Meetings

At the first Development Review Meeting, present the approved Design Document and the first stage of the portal—whatever you have developed so far. As the iterations move forward, you will get to the finer details of the site, with permissions being applied at the final iteration.

Remember *TIKI* point 4: INVOLVEMENT! Here is an opportunity to build excitement—you are creating their portal right before their eyes—so get them involved. Engage the users, remembering that people support what they have helped to build. Create a collaborative environment where people work together effectively to develop solutions. Try to be truly and actually *excited* about the discussion and not just give it lip service. Your enthusiasm will go a long way to engage the users and make the process fun. (More on this in **Chapter 6 – User Engagement** (page 53).

Capturing Notes

Always have your notebook open on the table so you can quickly write notes during the meeting and update the Design Document later. Or, if you are a good-enough typist and good at multitasking, you can update the Design Document live in the meetings, but this does take some practice. If you have someone capable and fast, recruit them as *scribe* to update the Design Document live in the meeting.

Lots of interaction still happens at this stage. It is not a case of saying "No, the Design Document says this, so it can't change." Remember what we said in the design phase, "Yes, we can and will continue to change." Incremental change is embraced throughout the project and is a key part of the *SharePoint in Practice* strategy.

Facilitating Meetings

As you run meetings, you will find that people are generally engaged, open, and creative, but sometimes the team includes a person who tends to go off on tangents or gets into too much detail.

Keep in mind that many people have trouble reading the Design Document and understanding what it's supposed to say, especially if they're not familiar with SharePoint. They may not have fully understood what was proposed in the Design Phase, and now that they see the live portal, they might say, "Oh! That's not what I meant" or "Hey! I see now, but can you do this?"

In these cases, it helps to make time for individual meetings as required (this is another reason to wait a few weeks between meetings). For example, the HR department may have specific, detailed requirements for a job posting list. If the rest of the design team doesn't need to be involved in the detailed design of that list, it makes sense to have a separate call or face-to-face meeting with the HR team member(s). Based on that special meeting, update the Design Document and start prototyping for presentation to the entire team.

In each meeting, present changes in the Design Document, then bring up the current portal-under-development to methodically walk the team through it. Refer to the Design Document as required without overly interrupting the flow. You might say, "*Here's that staff communications list we talked about. Notice we click here to add a new item, and we can enter the target audience. We can select Finance, for example. Now when we go to the finance department page, we see that new communication there. Does that make sense? Is this what we want it to do? Any questions or comments?*"

Remember to refer frequently to the Portal Purpose Statement and use it to keep asking, "*Are we on track? Is this accomplishing what we said we were going to accomplish?*"

Lastly, start and end your meetings on time. Respect people's time and they will respect yours.

Implementing Permissions

Implementing SharePoint permissions can be complex and confusing. This difficult task is greatly simplified thanks to our work on and preparation of the Design Document's *permissions plan*.

Permissions is the last big thing you do

The application of permissions is left until the last iteration in the development phase for several reasons:

1. *Avoid having to redo permissions.* Leaving permissions to the end means there are fewer moving parts. Most of the objects have been defined by then and built to the level where we are confident our design is not going to change much.

2. *Permissions can be difficult to understand.* To help your team learn, introduce the topic of permissions early in the process and discuss frequently. Repeating core permissions concepts and permissions guidelines will help people to understand permissions gradually. By the end of the development phase they will be more comfortable and ready to have productive conversations and make decisions around this important topic.

3. *Permissions can get in the way of testing and demonstration.* Because SharePoint permissions can cause your intranet to behave differently for different people, it can be confusing for the design team. For example, permissions trimming will hide lists and libraries and folders from anybody who doesn't have at least "read" permissions.

Build Permissions Groups

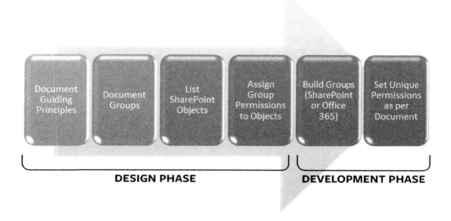

| Document Guiding Principles | Document Groups | List SharePoint Objects | Assign Group Permissions to Objects | Build Groups (SharePoint or Office 365) | Set Unique Permissions as per Document |

DESIGN PHASE   **DEVELOPMENT PHASE**

Figure 6 - Permissions Implementation Process

Start at the top level (root) site and add all permission groups as described in the Design Document. This is another place the split screen and copy/paste method serves you well. Note here we show and discuss examples using SharePoint Groups; if you are using Active Directory or Office 365 security groups, the approach will differ, but the concepts are the same.

The first permission group you will create is the SharePoint Administrator's group. In this instance, you must create the group and then go back and change the ownership of the group to itself. (Yes, read that again—it is correct, though recursive: the *SharePoint Administrators* group is owned by the *SharePoint Administrators* group.)

While creating SharePoint groups, make sure you change the *group owner* to your SharePoint administrator group. While adding a new SharePoint group, if you don't specifically assign ownership, the new group will be owned by *you,* the group creator. This is seldom appropriate. This is because, first, we plan to manage permissions by group, not by individual login. And second, in the future you may no longer be part of the project or the organization. If you're not around and you are listed as the group owner, Site Administrators won't be able to easily change group membership or event ownership. Only a Site Collection

Administrator is able to override that ownership. So to avoid future hassle in maintain the site, set that ownership now.

People and Groups · Change Group Settings ⓘ

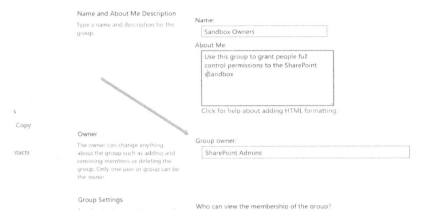

Figure 7 - Set Ownership to SharePoint Administrators Group

Notice that SharePoint automatically adds the group creator as a member of each group. Delete yourself right away. And while you're at it, if you have a list of group members from the Design Document or a global contact list, you can copy-paste them to conveniently populate the group membership right now, while you're in there. Otherwise make a plan to populate the group membership before go-live, or delegate this task.

Normally you will uncheck the "send an email invitation" option at this time. You can inform people of group membership and portal access in a much more user-friendly way, as part of go-live.

If you have a large list of groups to create, I suggest adding a *Status* column to the group table to assist you and your team in tracking which groups have been built and/to populated with user ids.

Work down the site hierarchy

Start at the top level and set permissions as you work your way *down the tree,* referring to the site structure diagram in the Design Document. Because of your planning and analysis, and this top-down approach, you will find that implementing permissions is a fairly quick process: The Design Document's "who can do what to what" table gives you a pretty easy *paint-by-numbers* approach. Do be careful, however, as it is important to set permissions correctly.

For example, let's say the Finance Department subsite will have unique permissions as per the below.

Securable object (site, list, library, folder, document, or item)	Description	Unique or inherited permissions?	Groups that need permissions	Permission level to assign (Read-only, Contribute, Full Control)	
Finance Subsite	The special site for the Finance Department	Unique	Group Name	Permissions	
			All Staff	Read	
			Finance Staff	Contribute	
			SharePoint Admins	Full Control	

Figure 8 - Example Permission Item for Finance Department

Navigate to the Finance subsite, which you previously created with *inherited* permissions. Navigate to the Site Settings/Site Permissions screen and break permissions inheritance (that is, create unique permissions). You will be left with the groups and permission levels as inherited from the parent site, and now able to modify the Finance site permissions, without affecting the parent site.

Now, while referring to the Design Document:

- remove any groups that should have no access to this object (not even permission to *Read*),

- edit the permissions level for any groups that are present but not correct, and

- grant access to new groups as required. (To be clear, the groups already exist—you are just giving them permissions to this object.)

Ideally, you will have two people working together setting permissions and/or double-checking afterward. Tracking different groups and permission levels can cause your eyes to cross. Check and test permission settings before content migration, and enlist a colleague or your development team to check it all again. This may seem tedious, but it can be very embarrassing if permissions are not set correctly and private documents are visible when they shouldn't be. To be extra cautious, you could create a mini test plan for your helpers along the lines of the table below.

Test Condition	Expected Behavior	Pass/Fail?	Comments
Click on this address	Should be able to add, edit, but not delete documents.		
Click *here*.	Should get a "not found" error		
Can you see *this folder*?	No folder should be visible		

Once permissions are applied, our development phase is pretty much complete except for one more Development Review Meeting where you will do a final walkthrough with permissions in place. Show the Design Team the permission settings (or a sample set at least) and confirm they match the Design Document.

Now get a formal sign-off that we are complete, from the Project Sponsor or their delegate. (See **Chapter 2**, page 7.)

At the end of the development phase, you will have a live company portal that matches the Design Document, and you will have quite a few people on your side who understand and accept the system.

CHAPTER 5

Pilot Testing

R UNNING A PILOT TEST OF THE NEW PORTAL—TESTING IT WITH A BROADER RANGE OF REAL USERS—IS A GREAT WAY TO IMPROVE PRIOR TO GO-LIVE. If project timelines are tight, you can skip the pilot test and just communicate with all staff about "the iterative approach we are taking." However, if you do have time, piloting has immense value, and you should embrace it wholeheartedly.

The pilot test process aligns nicely with our *SharePoint in Practice TIKI* philosophy:

- **Template-based.** See sidebar for the Pilot Plan.

- **Involve the users.** More people will use the portal and provide formal feedback.

- **Keep it simple.** The pilot test is not complicated.

TEMPLATE: Pilot Plan

Purpose: to clearly and concisely state why we are pilot testing, how it will run, and who is involved.

Audience: Project Sponsor, Project Manager, Pilot Team

Download templates at
https://lightlever.sharepoint. com/sites/book1

- **Iterate to improve.** You built the portal knowing it will be well-tested before go-live, and the portal and all associated materials will improve based on what you learn from the pilot.

The pilot phase is another opportunity to increase user engagement and to further refine the portal. It allows you to test all aspects of your system, including design, technical support processes, and end-user training.

How do we pilot test our new intranet portal?

Pilot Plan

First, let's make a plan.

Set a pilot period. Plan to pilot for three to six weeks. Anything longer than that and organizational interest will wane. Anything shorter and there won't be enough involvement or actual testing to get useful results.

Set clear goals for the pilot. Our main goal is to have real people use the system in real-world scenarios, so set a clear mandate for the pilot test and make sure that it is documented in the pilot plan. Get the plan signed off by the Project Sponsor.

Run the pilot as if you were actually rolling out the live portal. The pilot is a dry run: you're testing the system, but this is also an opportunity to test the roll-out procedures, training, and support processes. It's a mini go-live with a small audience. As with any roll-out, communication is a key part of the pilot. Make sure that the everyone understands that we are pilot testing an unfinished system, so some problems are likely. Ask for their help and their support. Ask them to identify where the portal falls short or might be improved. Ask them to be honest. And make sure you give them effective ways to report back to you, such as a standard email address or a suggestion box on the new portal itself. (See Part 2 of this book for the suggestion box design.)

> **TEMPLATE: Pilot Participants Kick-off Presentation**
>
> **Purpose:** To get the pilot team on board and moving in the right direction. Clarify their role, our expectations, and then provide the training in they need.
>
> **Audience:** Pilot Participants
>
> Download templates at **https://lightlever.sharepoint.com/sites/book1**

Give participants specific tasks to carry out during the pilot. It is not very effective to just say, "go ahead and use the system for four weeks." Depending on the interest and ability of the pilot users, you could ask them to do their normal jobs using the new system. Discuss this with your Design Team. If the portal is not loaded with content, this will not be practical. It is usually much more better to be able to say, "These are the tasks that we need you to perform."

The Pilot Team

With the plan in place, we can form a *pilot team*. These are the people who will be pilot testing the new (draft) portal.

You will start with the same team that has been working on design and development, your Design Team, and expand to include a variety of users with a variety of skillsets from across the organization. The broader the representation, the better your pilot test will educate you to produce a great portal. The key is to gather a small, representative sample across the organization, from front-line staff to managers. Make sure that everyone, including the executive, understands your Pilot Plan. Some of my clients have asked for staff time estimates for the pilot phase. If needed, first make it clear it is an estimate only (best guess, and every case will be different) and estimate:

> *Estimated Staff Hours = pilot duration in weeks X number of pilot participants X estimated hours per week.*

> If you use the *SharePoint in Practice* pilot plan template, the *estimated hours per week* is about five to 10 hours.

Pilot Activities and Activity Tracker

To capture the activity results and some comments along the way, you will create a pilot activity tracker to which the entire Pilot Team will contribute. This could be a simple Word or Excel document, or better yet, use a standard SharePoint Discussion Board. Each activity becomes its own discussion topic, with Alerts configured so pilot participants know when a new activity is added.

Examples of activities are listed below and in the Pilot Plan template. Note that the content and structure will vary. Be creative and make this as much fun as possible, with the pilot goals in mind.

1. Watch the "Overview Training" video [link]. What's one thing you learned? Post your comments in the Pilot activities tracker.

2. Update your Contact record to add your e-mail address and phone number to your profile.

3. In the Pilot Activities Tracker, list two ways to get to the portal home page (there are at least four).

4. If you haven't done so yet this week, enter a suggestion in the Suggestion Box. If you can't think of any actual suggestions, enter something silly like "Dr. Seuss was here."

5. Watch at least one support video. What did you learn? Leave your comments in the Pilot activities tracker.

6. Find a Word Document called Sneetches.docx. Open the document and fill in one of your favorite books in the box beside your name. How was this experience?

7. Watch the support video on Alerts [link]. Set an Alert on the <Library Name> Document Library to give you a weekly summary of changes made by other people. How might alerts be useful for you?

8. If you haven't done so yet this week, enter a suggestion in the Suggestion Box. If you can't think of any actual suggestions, enter something silly like "Let's have green eggs and ham in the break room." How was this experience? How can we improve the Suggestion Box?

9. Find the Governance Guide wiki pages. Scanning the Table of Contents, what here looks useful? What's missing?

10. If you haven't already done so, watch the video [link] on Document Versions. In the Sandbox, there is a Document Library called "Bartholomew's Files." How many versions of Oobleck.ppt are there? Edit the file to make a (fun?) change and save and close the PowerPoint. How was this experience?

11. Email one of the other pilot participants with an email entitled "My Favorite Food" and include an embedded link to a picture in the Foodstuffs [link] picture library. Hint: how to share files video [link]. Post your comments.

12. Notice the file "And to Think That I Saw It on Mulberry Street.doc". What's wrong with this file name? (HINT: read the Wiki page on File Naming Conventions.)

13. Can you change the way you see files in the "Bartholomew's Files" view? Is that permanent or temporary?

14. Co-authoring: Work with another pilot participant to try co-authoring with one of the documents in the sandbox. (See more about co-authoring here [link]). Note that some configurations of browser and MS Office may not support co-authoring, so please report your success/ challenges and versions.

15. In the sandbox document library, can you change the way files are displayed? (HINT: "Create View") Is this the way everyone will see these files or just you? Is this the default view, or not?

16. The Contact List has a number of Views defined. Choose the "Staff by Surname" view. Without counting, how many people have surname beginning with "D"?

17. What's the easiest way to get quick access to a project or library that you use frequently? How is this process for you?

18. Add your picture to your item in the contact list. Hint: watch the support video [here] to see how. Post your comments, or just post "done."

19. Imagine you are doing a lot of Project work. How will you make it easy to get back to the Projects site? There are at least three ways to create a shortcut to get to this page.

20. If you haven't done so already, create a new alert for the Announcements List. If you have an alert for this already, change the settings for this alert. How was this

experience for you? What specific ways might you use Alerts?

21. Modify the Graffiti Wall [link] wiki page to add "Kilroy was here" or whatever graffiti you want. (HINT: watch this how-to video [link]). How was this experience?

22. List at least two ways to see the latest files in the Finance document library. Who modified the most recent file? How do you know?

Evaluation

After the pilot test is complete, do a thorough evaluation to get further feedback and direction for Go-Live. This evaluation could be done by a simple survey or via more formal focus groups of about 10 pilot participants each. The survey is easy and cheap and could be done anonymously, which is an advantage. However, focus groups will provide more engagement and better learning. You get out what you put into a process—people will not provide as much useful information in a survey. In either case, via a survey or focus groups, you will ask:

- What did you find useful about the portal?

- What did you find frustrating or difficult?

- What would you suggest is important to change prior to releasing the portal to everyone?

- Any further comments?

- Note that your comments and ideas will be prioritized and may or may not create immediate action.

Document the results to learn from them. And be sure to close the loop with the pilot participants: make it clear that you respect their time and effort. Be sure to respond to every comment or recommendation that comes from the pilot participants. It might be a case of saying, "*Good idea. We don't have time (budget) to do that now, but it has been captured for possible future development,*" or you may be able to say, "*Yes, thank you for suggesting that; it will be done in this release.*"

Save all the learning, as this may be used in future releases or (in some cases) may form part of your training or FAQ materials.

CHAPTER 6

User Engagement

END-USER ENGAGEMENT IS THE PROCESS BY WHICH WE GET THE PORTAL USERS, AND POTENTIAL USERS, INVOLVED AND INTERESTED.

With engaged users who are truly excited about *their* new portal, the uptake of the system is higher, and the success of the project is more likely. Here are the key actions needed to get everyone on board. (Note that *Training* is an important factor in engagement; see **Chapter 9** (page 87) for the *SharePoint in Practice* training methods.)

Arguably, the biggest risk of failure or opportunity for success in your portal project depends on how involved (and even excited) the users are. Remember that *Field of Dreams* line, "If you build it, they will come"? That's only a movie, folks! People generally resist change of any kind, and a new company portal affecting the entire organization runs the risk of making *everyone* unproductive, unhappy, or both.

This is why the first "I" of our *SharePoint in Practice "TIKI"* is *Involvement*. By involving and engaging all stakeholders throughout the project, especially executive and end-users, the likelihood of a smooth project with good results is greatly increased. Put another way, it is essential to continually and effectively support everyone in embracing the new portal. This may feel a bit like you're delivering a sales pitch, but like any good sale, everyone wins!

So, get everybody involved early and often!

What is User Engagement?

Let's define "user engagement." A "user" is anyone who will be using the portal. And "engagement" here means getting people interested in the project, curious about the new system, and ultimately excited about how the portal (i.e., their cool new portal) supports them in doing their work.

This is not done by flipping a switch; it is a process that involves people, so it must be done carefully and methodically. A friend of mine who specializes in change management says that with any organization-wide change,

- 10% of the users will be enthusiastic about the change,

- 10% will be completely opposed, and

- 80% will be willing to consider the change might be for the better.

That's an interesting observation, using the good old 80/20 rule, but what was especially interesting is what he said next.

> *"So focus on the willing 80%. You don't need to worry about the enthusiastic 10% because they are already on board regardless. And the resistant 10%? They're not likely to change no matter what, so don't waste your energy there."*

TEMPLATE:
Communication Plan

Purpose: to clearly layout the steps and messaging of the communications around the portal development and roll-out

Audience: Steering Committee, Content Stewards, all staff

Download templates at
https://lightlever.sharepoint.com/sites/book1

Attitude is an important factor in how people approach change, so we try to build good feelings and positive expectations well in advance of users seeing the new portal.

How do we create a positive image and establish positive attitudes with users? The *SharePoint in Practice* method starts at the top.

Communications

User engagement is largely an exercise in communications. If you have corporate internal communication resources—a Communications department or perhaps Human Resources—be nice to them early and often, and ask them to help write, edit, and distribute messages.

All your communication will be grounded in the business problems that were discovered and defined in the design phase. (See **The Design Process** in **Chapter 3** (page 19).)

People become more engaged when their business problems are heard, documented, and acknowledged in a way that makes sense to them. Their ears perk up as if to say, *"Oh, okay, so maybe this portal thing* will *help me to do my work!"* You get people on your side; they're rooting for you because now you are working to make their job easier and their life better—you've shown you understand their pain and that you are working to ease it. This trust is valuable, and trust gained can be easily betrayed, so continue to listen and continue to refer to the business problems in ways that relate to your audience, and maintain an honest attitude of working for them.

> ## Change Management: The Larger Conversation
>
> User Change Management is a big, important topic— one too large to be addressed in this book. To learn more, consider these other books:
>
> - *Influencer: The New Science of Leading Change*, by Joseph Grenny and Kerry Patterson
>
> - *Leading Change*, by John P. Kotter
>
> - www.prosci.com

WIIFM: Think of your Audience

You may have heard that everybody's favorite radio station is WII-FM, *"what's in it for me?"*. There is truth to that. The only point of view anyone truly has is personal, and we are essentially self-interested. Keep this in mind to connect and engage and get people on board with the project.

You will be more successful engaging people when you can state their point of view in a way that demonstrates your understanding. For example, in introducing a staff training session, you may reiterate that *"One of the main issues we've heard—and need to solve—is that people are frustrated trying find and share vendor contact information. Do I have that right?"* If you were doing the same session for the executive team, you may say, *"I am told staff can't easily find contact details for preapproved vendors and that is causing inefficiencies, rework, and costly mistakes. Would you agree?"* Whether you're training, presenting, managing change, or doing design and development, refer to the business problems to be solved, and do it from the point of view of the audience at hand.

> ## A word in your ear...
>
> People feel appreciated when you listen to them. Time spent listening is never time wasted. When someone starts to tell you what is important to them in the new portal, take time to listen carefully and play back what you think you heard. In fact, make sure you factor that time into your project plan. The ideas, perspectives, and connections you can get from spontaneous, frank conversations are solid gold.
>
> You are not likely to be able to hear every voice in the organization, so make sure you listen carefully whenever you can.

Relationships—It's All Personal

A friend of mine is a buyer for a large company. He primarily works out of his home and travels a lot to meet clients. He makes a point of visiting the corporate office at least every week or two. He told me, *"I am a lot more productive at home, but I need those office relationships to get stuff done. The time spent in the office seeing people face-to-face and chatting means I'm more likely to hear 'yes' when I ask for a favor."*

An important part of user engagement is *relationships*. By connecting with and really listening to people, you start to develop relationships that support project success.

Know people's names and use them. Smile. Say hello when you walk into the office or meeting room. Create those connections!

You want as many people on your side as possible. When people are feeling connected to you and to the project, they will be more support-ive and more likely to spread positive comments about the project. Do whatever you can to create culture of acceptance and a culture open to change.

Don't be afraid to make it personal. During one project I was repeat-edly impressed with a member of the Design Team who kept coming up with great ideas—not just her own, but also collaboratively. During discussions, Donna would pipe up with, *"Yes, Jamie, I like that idea and what about we also...?"*, and as she spoke, people would be nodding and *seeing* the ideas take shape. At a Steering Committee meeting, I was able to show respect (and gain some) by briefly mentioning Donna's contributions: *"The team is performing well, and I've been particularly impressed by Donna. She has shown leadership and collaboration to produce some great ideas that we will definitely use."* This type of com-munication connects the executive with the grassroots of the project in a very simple way. And everybody loves a story. Help the executive to feel involved and excited, and they will be on your side when you need them.

Get out there and build those relationships!

Top-Down Engagement by the Numbers

Let's look at how you can involve and engage various groups to get them on your side.

Steering Committee

Everything runs downhill, so the engagement process starts at the top with senior management and leadership. This is another instance when a project Steering Committee is valuable and useful (see **Project Sponsor and Steering Committee** in **Chapter 2** (page 9)). This group spans and leads the organization, so their buy-in will support and influence the buy-in of many others.

For the Steering Committee meetings, show respect by making sure each meeting starts and ends on time. Display a professional attitude. "Professional" doesn't mean overly serious, however—use some tasteful, appropriate humor if you can. A silly joke or even just laughing a little during the meeting can lighten things up and wake up those stuffy executives.

Status Reports

The Steering Committee will be more engaged and more involved when they have a consistent, honest, and accessible view of how the project is coming along. While communicating with this group, keep in mind their need to solve business problems and improve the bottom line. And keep in mind they need to communicate with peers and answer to their superiors.

This group needs to be able to talk intelligently about the project, but they don't have a lot of time. Your regular Status Report is very valuable for this—a short, scheduled report in a standard format will allow these busy executives to keep a handle on the project at a glance. (Recall that the Status Report includes sections on Issues, Accomplishments, Plans, Budget, and Schedule.) See **Status Reporting** in **Chapter 2** (page 13) for more details.

Examples and Ideas

Early in the project, show the Steering Committee comparable company portals to trigger ideas. If you demonstrate similar systems (perhaps that you have built), they can better visualize what can be done and they may get excited about what we can create.

Ask the Steering Committee if there is an opportunity to present to a broader executive committee (CEO, Directors, Board Members—the more you can get in front of, the better). The Steering Committee will include some senior managers, so try to impress upon them the value of a presentation to the entire executive. Tell them that the portal touches everyone in the organization, so the broader the understanding of the project goals, the more successful you will be. You may be granted only a 10- or 15-minute time slot, so be organized, practiced, and on point. Provide an overview of the business problems to be solved, the high-level Project Plan, and if time permits, a sample portal site or two. If you can make this presentation happen, it is a great opportunity to engage and get buy-in throughout the organization.

Personal, Professional Communication

Don't be afraid to contact a Steering Committee member with specific questions or concerns. Be direct and brief when dealing with executives, unless you get indicators from them that they are the type of people who like to chat. A conversation might be as brief as, *"Hello, Margaret, it's Gerry Brimacombe calling about the portal project. Can you spare five minutes to talk?"* Margaret might say, *"Oh, yes, Gerry, how are you doing?"* or may go straight to," *Yes, what is it?"* or *"I can't talk right now."* From her response, we may chat a little and nurture the personal connection as well as the business at hand. When you can, politely bring the conversation around to the question or concern at hand. For example, *"The reason I'm calling is we're a little concerned about the engagement of the HR department. Bob and Alice haven't attended the last couple of meetings and since HR falls under your bailiwick, I wondered if there's anything you would like to do, or if I should follow up with their manager."* (Note that it is best to suggest a solution when presenting a problem.)

TEMPLATE: Executive Overview Presentation

Purpose: Give executive or management team an quick overview of the project and (possibly) example portal sites

Audience: Executive, Steering Committee, Executive, Management Team, CEO, etc.

Download templates at **https://lightlever.sharepoint.com/sites/book1**

Design Team

The *SharePoint in Practice* method has user engagement built in throughout the project. During the design phase, you will engage the Design Team through regular meetings. Listen to what they have to say, and ask for their advice, always reflecting back how their ideas may or may not address the project goals and business problems we are trying to solve.

When conducting design meetings, stay up-beat and enthusiastic:

- "I like that idea!"
- "Yes, we can include that in the help & support wiki page."
- "Yes, that totally supports our purpose statement."
- "That will save time, won't it?"
  - "Hmm, interesting idea… I wonder—how well does it align with this business problem?"

Stay curious and energetic with these folks, and you will find that people become engaged. They pay attention and feel like their ideas are being heard, and are excited to be co-creating the portal.

Food at the meetings can help. Don't treat snacks like a bribe, but you do want people to be functioning at their best, so if a meeting spans breakfast or a lunch hour or (hopefully never) dinner, then bring in some food so people are not distracted by hunger. It is not always necessary and can be a distraction.

User Community

It is difficult to engage *all* users, but let's see what can be done. Your access to the organization is mostly *indirectly* via the Design Team, the Steering Committee, and the Content Stewards.

We will discuss the **Content Steward Committee** in **Chapter 8** (page 81), but for now be aware that this is a committee of power-users supporting people using the portal at every level of the organization. Engage this group and get them excited about the project, and that enthusiasm will spread through the grassroots. Disappoint them, and disillusionment will spread instead.

We have a whole chapter on training, and it's worth mentioning here from a user engagement point of view. Training opportunities arise throughout the project. Teachable moments can happen in formal, organized, classroom training; ad hoc teaching while working with the Steering Committee; presenting to the board; or explaining the *quick edit view* to the Design Team. Any of these training opportunities should be grounded in the identified business problems to be solved and should reinforce the purpose statement whenever possible. When developing training or delivering it in a formal or an ad hoc fashion, keep in mind the learning outcomes and the behavioral changes that you want to occur. A desirable outcome of any training is increased user engagement. People fear what they don't understand, so help them to understand and to get excited about their new portal. This will help them to engage in the project and support its success.

Go-Live Contest

As part of releasing the portal to all staff, create a contest that encourages people to use the system. In the Go-Live Contest template, you will see this is a simple Q&A where most of the questions are easily answerable by using the portal.

Questions are designed to encourage and support users to:

- learn how to navigate the site,

- explore site structure,

- understand key lists and libraries,

- learn fundamental skills,

- know where to get help and support, and

- feel good about the new system.

TEMPLATE: Go-Live Contest and Training Survey

Purpose: Create a contest that encourages use of the new portal and helps people to understand it

Audience: All staff

Download templates at **https://lightlever.sharepoint.com/sites/book1**

The last point, "feel good about the system," is why the Go-Live Contest is here in the *User Engagement* chapter rather than under training.

We make this a *contest* to engage users from a different angle, generate some interest, and to reward people for their participation. Just by completing the Go-Live Contest, people are eligible to win a prize. Three to five winners are selected by a random draw from everyone who has completed the contest (regardless of their answers: we don't care if they "got it right," just that they've tried).

Get creative with the prizes. Check with the Communications Department, HR, or the Executive team to see if there is budget available for staff prizes, and what the policies are around them. Consider:

- Lunches or coffee cards from local eateries. This can be fun, and you could ask for donations in exchange for publicity.
- Hats or T-shirts printed with the logo and/or slogan of the new portal.
- Silly prizes like plush toys, "World's Greatest" mugs, or toy trophies.
- Time off work. This one is great if the organization permits it. The message becomes, "The new portal will save you so much time, you can leave at noon on Friday."

Recognition is, of course, something everyone loves. Make sure the winners are announced as much as possible, in meetings, in the corporate newsletter, mass email, and in the *News* section of the new company portal.

CHAPTER 7

Content Migration

H OW DO YOU LOAD EXISTING MATERIAL INTO YOUR NEW PORTAL? This is usually the hardest part of the project, and the tips here will make it a little easier. The biggest category of "content" to be migrated is "files and folders," so moving files to the portal prior to Go-Live is the focus of this chapter.

Content migration is complex, time-consuming, risky, and stressful. Usually source files are loosely or poorly organized, with limited structure and lots of duplication. Often we are dealing with a large (sometimes *very* large) volume: perhaps hundreds of thousands of files and folders, adding up to gigabytes or even terabytes to be moved. In addition to these practical points, there are emotional considerations: file servers hold many years of history that some staff cannot imagine leaving behind. And migration efforts can take many, many hours of staff time and attention, which can be daunting and depressing for the busy office worker. Luckily, we have some practical methods to address these challenges and manage migration.

Throughout the project we manage expectations, and migration is no exception. If management and staff *expect* that SharePoint is going to automatically solve all their content searching and file organization problems without a lot of planning and effort, you are being set up for failure.

Everyone must understand the risk of garbage in/garbage out (GIGO). If the file servers to be transferred to the new portal have been loosely managed and the material is disorganized, duplicated or out of date, then copying that into SharePoint will just create the same mess in a different place. You will be worse off in fact, because now you are dealing with web interfaces and metadata in an environment that is new to people. We strongly recommend you use the portal project as an impetus and encouragement to do a large-scale file clean-up *before* migration. This may be done partially before and partially after migration, but the more you can do *before*, the better.

One of my clients used an excellent analogy: she compared *migrating files* to *moving to a new apartment*—your old file servers or existing (old) portal and your new company portal is like your old and new apartment. When you are preparing to move your belongings, the more you can clean up beforehand, the better. Throw away the boxes you haven't opened since your last move. Donate that closet full of old sports equipment to charity before you start loading the truck. Every little thing you keep is going to add to the effort and cost of moving. When you arrive at the new apartment and unbox the old towels and chipped teacups that you couldn't bear to toss out, you now have to handle every one and find a place to put it; every item takes a little attention. There is a cost of time and effort to load, unload, *and* store every item. Keep this analogy in mind and share it repeatedly with your migration team. Every bit of clean-up you can manage now makes the job easier, faster, and cheaper, and the new "housing" for your files is less cluttered, easier to organize, and a better place to live and work.

Prepare for Content Migration

As mentioned, the migration of files to the new portal is the most complex part of the project. We will use carefully selected tools and rely heavily on knowledgeable staff or Subject Matter Experts[4] to assist with this work.

---

4   The term "Subject Matter Expert" or SME (pronounced "smee") is a term commonly used to identify a person who knows a lot about their business domain or subject matter. We rely heavily on SMEs to understand their department's workings and files and to help prioritize and organize what is to be migrated. Your Migration Team should be SMEs.

The Migration Plan

Not surprisingly, the first step is to write a plan ... and even less surprising, we have template for that.

This phase of the project starts early to give the Migration Team time to clean-up content (files, emails, lists, etc.) to be migrated. It begins with a brief analysis and planning exercise to determine what needs to be moved, who will perform the work, what guidelines should be followed, and how the content will be migrated. Migration analysis and planning will start during the Design Phase of the project, and actual migration work can take place in parallel with developing and pilot testing the portal.

TEMPLATE: Content Migration Plan

Purpose: To describe and agree upon the steps to migrate content to the new portal, including who does what when.

Audience: Management, Migration Team, Project Manager

Download templates at **https://lightlever.sharepoint. com/sites/book1**.

You may be moving or copying content from a variety of sources. You might have files on a server, libraries and lists on an old SharePoint site, or documents in Dropbox, personal drives or in email. Files (documents) and folders are the largest and most obvious focus of a migration, but the move could include: document libraries, lists such as calendars or contacts, photos, etc. Catalog these, understand them, and consider migration strategies for each one.

Review the Migration Plan template. Notice the plan shows all the steps required to move content from existing sources to the new portal, starting with some guiding principles.

EXAMPLE

Migration Guiding Principles

Principle	Explanation
1. Files to be migrated come from the existing SharePoint site, <site name>, and file servers, <server names or drive letters>, and are migrated to the new SharePoint site.	This guiding principle is just to list the content source(s) and destinations at a high-level and exclude any content sources that are not in scope. More detail can be included in the plan.
2. We recognize migration is a difficult and daunting task. As such, we will do our best and have a plan to improve and complete any missing data over time.	This principle is to encourage the users to relax and engage with the process. Let them know that you understand this is difficult, that you know they're busy, that although we're going to do our best, the results won't be perfect, and it is going to improve over time. Be realistic about the process and set expectations. Let them know that you're going to need a lot of help from the users and from subject matter experts in the various departments to provide advice regarding the content to be retained, migrated, and tagged.
3. We will use migration tools <list tools> to help the process.	State up front whether you will be using a migration tool such as Sharegate, Metalogix, Excel, or whatever to help with the process.
4. Reliable backups are important. We will create them or ensure they already exist and are restorable before trimming content.	Backups are always a good idea. Let's be explicit about their existence and know that we can access them if needed. I have seen many organizations that create backups regularly but don't test their ability to *restore* from those backups. Don't assume the backup is usable; test to be sure.
5. We will follow file- and folder-naming rules.	Following file-naming rules and conventions is important during migration. This is an opportunity to rename files, shorten folder and file names, remove invalid characters, standardize, etc. It may even be technologically *necessary* to make these changes (e.g., special characters are not valid in a SharePoint library). Again, this can be a daunting but worthwhile process. Migration tools can help here.

Principle	Explanation
6. Information Architecture, including metadata fields and their defaults, will be defined in advance of loading content into SharePoint.	We design libraries, folders, lists, and metadata when we design the portal. This structure is defined prior to migration so files can be placed and tagged appropriately. Even if you can't tag automatically, you will need to set metadata and/or folder structures before you go-live, so defining the structure (architecture) is a prerequisite.
7. Only files modified <cutoff date> or newer are considered for migration. This is called the migration cutoff date. There may be some exceptions to this rule.	Defining a *migration cutoff date* can make migration easier for everyone. Remember the *moving to a new apartment* analogy? A cutoff date is a great way to make it clear that *we're going to limit how much we move*. Usually we migrate two to five years of content to SharePoint; everything prior to the cutoff date stays behind. There may be exceptions to this date. One of my clients had a migration cutoff date of 18 months, but there were two large ongoing projects that had started two years ago. They wanted all project documents to be available on the portal, so these project files were identified as exceptions to the rule.
8. After content is migrated, the associated source (drive, list or library) becomes a read-only historical archive and may be deleted after 90 days.	Depending on the specific situation, after content is migrated, the associated source (the file server, list, library, etc.) may be set to *"read only"* and become a historical archive. In this case, we don't *move* content into SharePoint, we *copy* it over and keep it available at the source as a fallback. More on this in the Migration Method section below.

Migration Analysis and Planning

Planning is fundamental to the content migration process, and the way to get started is to identify and understand all content sources.

Even while designing the portal, a good understanding of what needs to be migrated can be very useful. This information can inform your project plan and your design, so start early.

Find out where content is now stored. List the file servers, existing SharePoint sites, and other sources that may exist.

> **TEMPLATE:** Content Migration Checklist
>
> **Purpose:** to identify what needs to be migrated, and track who is responsible and the migration status.
>
> **Audience:** Migration Team
>
> Download templates at
> **https://lightlever.sharepoint.com/sites/book1**

Be sure to ask about other storage such as Dropbox, Box, Google Drive, external hard drives, email, department-specific servers, and *anything else that might need to be found on the portal.* If our design and purpose dictate that the portal is a *one-stop-shop to find corporate information,* then all these myriad sources should be consolidated through the migration process.

Take some time to look at the content sources. Get a sense of the structure, content type, and volume. For file servers, you may use the Excel-based tool to count files, folders, and gigabytes, or you may use a migration tool such as Sharegate, file system commands and rough estimating techniques. The structure of the existing content *may or may not* dictate and inform the structure of the new portal. Use the existing architecture as a springboard, not a specification, and discuss with your Design Team.

Tag your content sources with named Content Owners—your corporate content experts (SMEs). Now the migration team starts to take shape.

> **TEMPLATE: File Migration (Excel) Tool**
>
> **Purpose:** to analyze directories for file size, number. To look for path and filenames that are too long, and for special characters. To rename files.
>
> **Audience:** Migration Team
>
> Download templates at **https://lightlever.sharepoint.com/sites/book1**

EXAMPLE

Content Source Listing

Content Source	Size	Migration Notes	Content Owner(s)
J: drive	Approx 775 GB 58,910 files 307 folders	Primarily used to store finance and executive files Managed by a small group; quite tightly managed with little duplication or redundancy Contains sensitive information; not for general consumption All content will need to be migrated, regardless of age	Bob McSamson, Director of Finance Dan Sabor, Executive Assistant

Content Source	Size	Migration Notes	Content Owner(s)
K: drive	Approx 1,075 GB 678,000 files 891 folders	Used to store communications files Contains many very large video files and some AutoCAD, Adobe Illustrator, and other graphics materials. Some of these files may be too large for SharePoint limits. Need to consider alternatives. Subfolder "OLD" is a dump from a previous employee and has been kept "just in case." Likely can be left behind as an archive	Susan Pronata, Director of Communications Danny Dracksen, Communications Manager
Drop-box/ Share	Approx 47 GB 127 files 3 folders	Used to share files with partners and contractors. Will be moved to "extranet" component of portal Retain existing structure to reduce impact on partners Review permissions with team before Go-Live	Susan Pronata, Director of Communications Sam Pachinko, Board Liaison

The Migration Team

While developing the plan, assemble a team of staff members who will assist with migration. There's a lot of work involved in file clean-up and migration, and you will need help. Working from the content source list, get advice from your Steering Committee and Design Team to recruit the help you need. This will include garnering approval for people to put time and energy into content migration (e.g., permission from their manager).

This is another instance where the Content Steward model (see **Chapter 8 – Practical Governance** (page 77)) will serve you well. The Content Stewards are the perfect group to help with migration. This group is already getting extra SharePoint exposure and training, and you already have a relationship with them.

The migration team members should have technical skill, and good understanding of the content to be migrated. For example, the person who will lead the migration of the Finance department's content should understand the structure and content of Finance folders and files. That doesn't mean they must have all the answers; they need to be able to check with colleagues in their department if there are questions regarding which projects or documents should or should not be migrated. They should also have good relationships with the managers and staff in their area.

While recruiting the team, acknowledge and communicate that file clean-up and the migration itself may require a considerable time commitment. Share the Migration Plan and Guiding Principles. Team members' managers will want to know how much time (how many working hours) will be required. The amount of time required depends on the quantity of content being migrated, but I always try to estimate high and hope to come in lower. Specific estimates will depend on the process chosen.

The Migration Process – You Have Options

Let's talk about some different ways to manage the migration.

"Migrate as Needed" Process

The first method is to build the portal and when it is live set the file source locations to "read only." As part of Go-Live, communicate to all users that whenever they need a file, the process is to look for it on the portal, and if not found there, they should pull it off the old file source and save it to the appropriate location on the new portal. Once saved, it is "read/write" as per your permissions plan. So, until a file is specifically needed by someone and copied over, it remains "read only" in its old location. So, a file remains "read only" in its old location until is specifically needed by someone, and then copied over.

Use this approach when you don't have time do much up-front migration work and are willing to ask all users to do more work over an extended period. This works best when users are technically capable and able to understand how and where to move files.

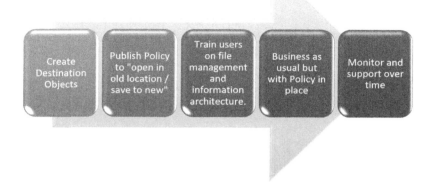

Figure 9 - Migrate as Needed Process

This approach is simple and easy to plan and execute, and it is great that only active files are moved to the portal, slowly and methodically. The downside, which usually rules out this process, is that it adds uncertainty and overhead to your users' day-to-day work processes—uncertainly because they are not sure where they will find their content, and overhead to search and move as required. This can be frustrating for people to constantly interrupt their work to look for documents on the portal *and then maybe* on the old file server. At first, they will find most documents on the old server, but over time, more and more files are on SharePoint.

Also consider that the SharePoint structure and metadata must be well documented and clearly communicated. All users need to be trained so they know where and how to save documents on the new site. (This is necessary anyway, but arguably, more training is required to support them loading files in rather than finding migrated files and using them).

Your sparkly new portal will quickly become a mess if you don't have the structure well-defined and file transfers carefully monitored. Sometimes it is better to move documents in bulk (see below) because portal structure and file destinations are well known by few people and easier to manage.

Finally, note that you will need to keep your source files around for some time, most likely a year or more.

"One and Done" Process

Another approach to migration is "one and done," or the big bang approach. Here you will copy and paste all your content from your old file server(s) into the new portal, with little analysis or restructuring.

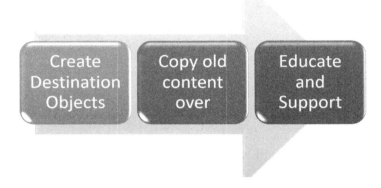

Figure 10 - One and Done Method Process

In choosing this migration method, consider the state and number of your content sources. As mentioned earlier, often file servers may be poorly organized or at least not organized in the way you want your portal to be. You are risking what's called a *"garbage in, garbage out"* process. If you have poor structure on your servers, you will just replicate the mess that already exists, and make things worse.

Communicate during the planning phase that the migration process is an opportunity to clean up your content, and most content does need cleaning up. This method is a pretty easy migration—largely a cut and paste—but it is not usually feasible. You could cut, paste, and then clean up in the portal afterwards, but once in SharePoint, it is more awkward to organize and delete files (compared to Windows file management and file explorer tools), and you could end up causing yourself more work and frustration.

The SharePoint in Practice Process: Staging

The approach we prefer to use takes a little more management but the results are better. Hearkening back to the moving apartments analogy, thoroughly clean and organize in the old apartment first, and then only move the cleaned-up and minimized stuff.

There are a few ways to do this; use the ideas here and adapt the Migration Plan to what will work for you and your people.

Figure 11 - Migration Using Staging Flow

First create a *Staging Area* on a file server accessible to the migration team. This will be used exclusively by the Migration Team for clean-up and preparation. Structure the Staging Area with folders that correspond to your main portal objects (mostly document libraries). The Staging Area is just temporary—once you have copied content to SharePoint, it can be deleted.

We then roughly copy all content to be migrated into the staging area and clean it up there. We might dump in content from several file servers, Dropbox, Google Drive, and other sources. In staging, your Migration Team will delete redundant material, rename files and folders, and move content around to correspond to destination libraries in the new portal.

Here's a place the migration cutoff date comes in handy. Only source content newer than the cutoff date, along with any exceptions, is copied to staging. Migration tools can help (see below). Keep a record in the Content Migration Checklist of the date and time you copied files to staging; you will need this later.

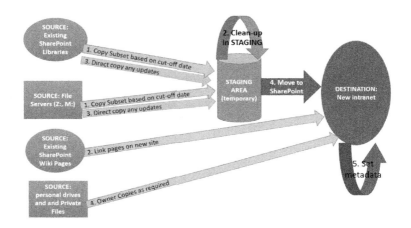

Figure 12 – Migration with Staging Detailed Process

A benefit of working with a staging area is the migration team can clean up without disturbing the source files or disrupting their colleagues' day-to-day work. They are not moving and renaming live files, just grabbing a copy of them and then working with that copy. Consider what might need to happen during migration. Any of these activities could be quite disruptive to the day-to-day work of the business:

- renaming files and folders to follow naming conventions
- flattening folder structures
- deleting duplicated and redundant content
- deleting old content
- completely moving things around

Plan at least a few weeks of focused effort to allow your migration team to organize and tidy content in the staging area. It may be tempting to allow more time, and for complex migration that would be wise, but also try to keep a sense of urgency. The clean-up is unpleasant work that people tend to avoid.

Once staging reorganization is complete, and prior to copying into SharePoint, search for changes in the content sources. Refer to the Content Migration Checklist for dates and list any source content that has changed since the copy to staging. These "recent edits" need to be copied into the staging area and named and placed appropriately. This may seem onerous on the surface, and it is largely a manual process, but it is usually a smaller set of data than you would expect, especially if you have a short staging time.

At this point, staging is clean and structured, thanks to the work performed by the Migration Team. Now let's move that content into the portal.

The move from Staging into SharePoint may be done using drag-and-drop with Windows Explorer view, with copy commands after mapping a drive to SharePoint, or by using a migration tool such as Sharegate or Lightlever's Excel-based tool.

If you do decide to use manual methods (our Excel tool or drag-and-drop) to move files into SharePoint document libraries, note that any SharePoint file version history is lost. Also, the standard *Modified By* and *Modified* (date) fields are set to the name of the person who copied the files and the date they did it. This is not ideal and is an important reason you may opt to spend the money to purchase a migration tool.

If you are not using a migration tool, metadata is set after the migration is completed. The Migration Team members—who are the subject matter experts and responsible for migrating the content—have a task, post-copy, to set the metadata in SharePoint. A couple of tricks make this step easier.

1. As far as possible, specify default metadata[5] prior to copying. If you have managed metadata, you can set the default metadata at the folder level. Then when you upload files, the metadata will automatically be filled in.

2. Get Migration Team members to use document library Quick Edit (datasheet) views to fill in metadata. This takes time but works well, especially with managed metadata.

3. Ask people to set metadata as they open files. Similar to the Migrate as Needed method, this has pros and cons.

4. Other methods using PowerShell or commercially available migration tools.

---

5 Here's one article on how to set default column metadata: **https://www.collaboris.com/how-to-set-default-column-values-on-a-document-in-sharepoint/**.

Migrating Non-File Content

The discussion in this chapter is focused on migrating *files*, which is usually 95% of what you will migrate. If you need to migrate SharePoint lists, such as contact lists, calendars or custom lists, the best way to go is using a professional tool such as Sharegate. If you don't have budget for such a tool, you may be able to:

- export your list to Excel and then import into a new list,

- to migrate a small number of items, copy and paste into a data-sheet view in the new list, or

- save your list (including content) as a template and recreate it in the new location[6].

These methods are not 100% reliable, but they may work for you.

A Word about Migration Tools

For large migrations, there really is little choice but to employ a tool such as Sharegate, AvePoint, or Metalogix. This book won't get into detail about these tools, but any good migration tool will support the methods detailed above. Here is an excellent article on the subject: **https://collab365.community/sharepoint-comparison-matrix-for-3rd-party-migration-tools/**.

You might not need a third-party migration tool to help with file analysis and migration. Lightlever has developed an Excel workbook that, though a bit "Excel Technical," allows us to analyze file listings and migrate files (for example) *only newer than X date* or *only smaller than Y size*. These capabilities may be cost saving and almost certainly will save time and effort for the Migration Team. That tool is available at **sharepointinpractice.com**.

---

6   This article explains how: **https://en.share-gate.com/blog/copy-list-in-sharepoint-to-office365-tool**

CHAPTER 8

Practical Governance

YOU PLAN TO USE YOUR PORTAL FOR A LONG TIME, SO HOW WILL YOU MAKE SURE IT STAYS USEFUL? Governance helps everyone to approach the portal consistently, so your content and structure doesn't quickly degrade into chaos. This chapter provides a simple governance framework that you can adapt to your needs.

Overview

Here, *Governance* refers to rules, guidelines, and processes whereby a SharePoint portal is managed. For example, it includes who can create sites and why, how lists and libraries are modified, how permissions are managed, and the rules around page layout or color schemes.

We will develop a *Governance Guide*. You may have seen reference to SharePoint Governance Plans. We call our version a *guide* rather than a *plan*: The word "guide" is a bit softer and sets the tone for something that advises and supports, as opposed to a hard set of rules in a rigid plan. If you want to give your governance more of a sense of authority, absolutely, go ahead and can call it the Governance Plan or Portal Governance Policies. The content will be much the same, but you will write it with a more directive style.

Developing Governance

You will keep the guide simple, per the *SharePoint in Practice* philosophy and repurpose some of the materials we have already created.

Some content for the Governance Guide can be lifted directly from the Design Document. The permissions section slots in nicely, including the guiding principles, permissions groups, and the entire "who can do what to what" table. You will need to flesh this out a bit—adding rules about who manages permissions and how. This information is not in the Design Document but should be included in the Governance Guide.

> **TEMPLATE:**
> **Governance Guide**
>
> **Purpose:** Starting point for all governance rules and guidelines
>
> **Audience:** All users, but especially Content Stewards and Site Owners/managers
>
> Download templates at
> **https://lightlever.sharepoint.com/sites/book1**

Other material to lift from the Design Document includes the descriptions of each list and library. These sections were developed to support the design and build and are useful in the Governance Guide so that anyone managing the site has the background and list/column/view details they need.

A key part of the governance of your site will be the roles and committees that manage decisions and changes to the site. This material may be borrowed from Terms of Reference documents developed earlier for the Steering Committee and the Content Stewards Committee.

Governance Guide Components

The following are common components of any governance guide:

1. **Roles and responsibilities** – Who can do what in the site, spelled out in simple terms that anyone can understand. Who manages permissions? Are there special rules so Content Stewards manage permissions for their areas? Who can add or change metadata fields

and content types? Who can modify lists and libraries, including fields and views?

2. **File naming conventions** – What are the rules for naming folders and files? Do we separate words with spaces, dashes or underscores, or do we use CamelCaseNamingConventions?

3. **Permissions for lists and libraries content** – For each list and library, who can read, contribute, or control content (files, folders, and items)? As mentioned above, this is largely lifted from Design Document.

4. **Creation and deletion of sites, lists, and libraries** – Who can add and remove SharePoint objects? What are the rules and approvals required?

5. **Management of wiki pages** – Who can edit, add and remove site pages (wiki pages)? What are the rules and approvals required? Does this differ department by department or page by page? Can page layouts be changed?

6. **Graphics standards** – What are the standards for colors and logos? Are there specific page layouts that must be followed?

7. **Change Management** – Who/how do we manage change to the portal? Is there an approval process, and if so, for all changes or just major changes? Can certain people change things in certain areas—for example, are Content Stewards permitted to manage permissions and wiki pages for their department?

Governance Implementation

The Governance Guide should be a set of wiki pages. You can build these pages directly in the Site Pages library, or consider a dedicated wiki library if you are going to create a dynamic table of contents (as demonstrated in the example in Part 2 of this book). In the latter case you will need a customized wiki library with some metadata added.

The Governance Guide is managed by the Governance Committee, and any changes must be approved by a quorum there. Make approved changes directly in the wiki so it is always current, and version history is automatically tracked.

Link to the Governance Guide from your help page, refer to it in training, and include it in the portal's top menu.

Governance Committee

The top layer of governance is the *Governance Committee*. If you had a Steering Committee to guide portal development, then those members are great candidates for the Governance Committee. If changes are required to the Governance Guide, or major changes to the site, the Governance Committee must approve them.

> **TEMPLATE:**
> **Governance Committee Terms of Reference**
>
> **Purpose:** Define and describe the roles and expectations of the Portal committee
>
> **Audience:** Management Team, Content Stewards, Project Manager, all users
>
> Download templates at
> **https://lightlever.sharepoint. com/sites/book1**

Whereas Content Stewards organize, coordinate, and even execute small changes, any significant changes must be centrally managed. Content Stewards make recommendations, via their Chair, to the Governance Committee. The Governance Committee will review those recommendations and decide if we proceed or not. This provides a reasonable layer of oversight to manage changes to the portal.

To ensure continuity, the chair of the Content Stewards committee is a member of the Governance Committee. The Governance Committee should contain members of the Communications department, IT, HR, and Finance. If there are any other large departments or divisions in your organization, make sure they are represented. For example, one of my clients has a Customer Service division that employs 70% of the corporate staff. This division gets extra representation on the Content Stewards committee and a seat on the Governance Committee. It is important to make sure that such a large group is represented and involved.

The Governance Committee generally meets quarterly but may meet more frequently if the portal is undergoing extensive changes.

Content Steward Committee

As evidenced by how often they are referenced in this document, the Content Stewards committee is an important team. This committee, sometimes called *SharePoint Power-Users*, is ideally formed with at least one representative per department, division, or geographical area of your user group. These people are expected to understand the portal architecture, and the governance guide, and should be proficient with SharePoint. This is not normally a full-time role, but an additional responsibility of 5 to 10 hours per week.

> **TEMPLATE:** Content Stewards Terms of Reference
>
> **Purpose:** Define and describe the roles and expectations of the Content Stewards committee
>
> **Audience:** Management Team, Content Stewards, Project Manager, all users
>
> Download templates at
> **https://lightlever.sharepoint. com/sites/book1**

As in any committee, the Content Stewards need a chair. The chair will coordinate and facilitate the meetings and will be the primary channel of communication between the Content Stewards and the Governance Committees.

The chair may be you. As the project manager leading the development of the portal, it may make sense for you to transition into the operational role of leading the Content Stewards.

Committee membership can and will change. You want people who are engaged and involved. In the normal course of business, people retire and change positions, so from time to time, you may find certain areas are under-represented or less engaged than you need. So, include a process in the Governance Guide whereby members can be recruited to join, or removed from, the Content Stewards group.

Content Steward Role

Content Stewards are a two-way conduit for information flow. They provide deskside training and support to help the users, and gather and report issues and ideas.

EXAMPLE

Content Steward Duties and Responsibilities
(*excerpt from Terms or Reference*)

Individually and collectively, Content Stewards:

- field questions from peers, answering when they can, and facilitating finding solutions when they cannot answer

- raise ideas, issues, and improvements, and bring to <Project Manager> or the Governance Committee meeting

- communicate to those around them; train and support users

- help govern the Portal; proactively check sites and libraries for Governance compliance

- responsible for understanding and "owning" the content for their area

- require more SharePoint training (and aptitude) than an average user

- understand permissions and metadata

- as required, perform or coordinate metadata tagging and moving content

- share discoveries, learning, and time with each other and with their colleagues

- review, provide feedback, approve, and maintain SharePoint Governance Plan

- monitor SharePoint usage to uncover opportunities for improvement – new ideas and best practices – and review possible modifications to Governance Plans and best practices

- govern ongoing enhancements to SharePoint ensuring that initiatives are relevant to staff and appropriately prioritized

continued on next page

---

continued from previous page

- be the core advocates for SharePoint, communicating new and improved initiatives to all staff throughout the organization
- keep aware of technical developments affecting Share-Point
- participate in meetings and activities required by the Committee

---

The Content Stewards are your "ears on the ground," relaying issues and ideas to the development team or the Governance Committee. Since Content Stewards are recruited as regular staff from specific business units, they are on site and on level to support their peers and hear any issues. When you can effectively gather feedback such as "finance is frustrated with entering metadata," this is valuable information that can inform site governance (as well as training, support, and design). The Content Steward role personalizes this feedback loop and allows you to effectively manage your portal in a more collaborative fashion.

Content Stewards support governance by knowing the site structure (the information architecture) and supporting and reminding users to follow it.

Content Stewards also may support governance by managing permissions for their business area. By giving permission management capabilities and responsibilities to the Content Stewards you de-centralize that control. For example, additions, changes, or deletions to user access in the Finance department are managed by the Finance department Content Steward(s). Keeping this control close to the source can create a more responsive site management structure and better governance.

Usually Content Stewards maintain divisional home pages or landing pages for their department. The administrative overhead of this task is reduced when a Content Steward can directly update pages for their business area, rather than using a request-confirm-do-publish-check loop where wiki pages are managed by a central body like Communications or IT.

A key to this structure and the Data Steward role is the permissions plan "who can change do what to what" as developed in the Design Document and replicated in the Governance Guide.

Content Steward Communications

Content Stewards should meet at least monthly. See the side bar for a sample agenda for a Content Stewards meeting.

Note that extra SharePoint training is both a requirement and a privilege of being on the Content Stewards committee. See **Chapter 9 – Training** (page 87) for more detail.

The Content Stewards have a key role in training and support—they are on the front line with users. Try to nurture that and remind everyone, from the executive to the administrators and staff, to approach the Content Stewards with suggestions and for support. Raise the visibility of the Content Stewards by promoting these folks as your first avenue for SharePoint help and encouraging each Content Steward to *actively* embrace their role. Ask the Content Stewards to approach their users to offer help, not just wait for the users to come to them.

> **TEMPLATE: Content Stewards Active Meeting Agenda**
>
> **Purpose:** to plan and capture the discussion for any given Content Stewards meeting.
>
> **Audience:** Content Stewards Group
>
> Download templates at **https://lightlever.sharepoint. com/sites/book1**

Acknowledge that Content Stewards will not be able to answer every question posed, so design the support structure so they can bring questions back to committee meetings. They may also find answers to user questions themselves (e.g., by Google or sandbox testing) and then share the answer with the group as well as the user who asked. To support this discussion and share information between meetings in an efficient manner, a Content Stewards Discussion Board can be useful. Depending on your corporate culture, this discussion board may be private to Content Stewards but it is usually public so all staff can learn from the shared questions, ideas, and information.

Governance and Training

It's useful to notice the overlap between governance and training. Of course, governance is about the roles, policies, guidelines and procedures for governing or managing your site. To make sure people use the site consistently and correctly, defined rules are needed, *and people need to know those rules*. So, look to your governance guide to inform your training material. And watch for opportunities where training material may be referenced in the governance guide. For example, a governance page describing the rules around managing permissions might include a link to a support video showing how to add and remove users. To truly empower your users and make the Governance Guide useful, look for opportunities to include these training linkages wherever it makes sense to do so.

CHAPTER 9

Training

THAT FANCY NEW CAR IS USELESS, EVEN DANGEROUS, UNTIL YOU LEARN HOW TO DRIVE IT. You can't enjoy the cool breeze if you can't turn on the air conditioning. Your portal is the same—we don't consider the project a success until people are using it happily, and to make that happen, training is critical. This chapter describes practical training tools and techniques that will get everybody shifting gears with excitement.

Chapter 6 (page 53) was about User Engagement. Training involves and excites the users while enabling them use their portal well. Don't expect people to figure out the new tools on their own. Some may succeed without your help, but most would not, and that "trying to figure it out" process can be an exercise in user frustration that you should avoid at all costs.

The obvious purpose of training is to ensure users can and will use their new system effectively. Also, recognize that good training includes a bit of public relations (PR): training helps people accept the new system, piques their interest, and may even get them *excited* about how the portal can improve their work life. Keep this in mind as you design and especially *deliver* your training programs. Keep up-beat and positive— and if you can add a bit of energy and *enthusiasm*, that will serve you well. I cautiously refer to this as "selling in the classroom." Make sure you shine a light on the best aspects of the new system, talk about how it meets their stated business needs, and present with a smile on your face and a spring in your step!

The Training Plan

Develop a training plan that is short, practical, and actionable—as always, *KISS*. A simple training plan may be nothing more than a table describing who needs what training and when. Here is an example.

Topic	Structure	Learning Outcomes	Audience	Timing
Executive Overview (See **Executive Overview Presentation**)	Brief face-to-face overview presentation 15 to 30 minutes	Understand how the portal can benefit their business, in general Understand how the portal will support their business, specifically Understand basic terminology and structure Support the portal project key initiative Support the portal as a key business system	Executive leadership team	Prior to go-live
Support Videos	5 – 10 minute screen capture with voice over	Understand and be able to apply specific, useful topics to effectively use the portal	All users	Developed and posted before go-live Viewable by users on demand, as required

Topic	Structure	Learning Outcomes	Audience	Timing
Content Stewards Training (See **Content Stewards Training 1** and **Content Stewards Training 2**)	Hands-on instructor-led face-to-face (or online) At least 2 x half-day sessions	Understand their role as a Content Steward Understand the Governance Guide Be able to perform Content Stewards' duties well Understand permissions Understand site Information Architecture Understand the Design Document Be confident to support others Know where to get help	Content Stewards	Prior to Go-Live
Site Administrator Training (See **SharePoint Administrator Training**)	Hands-on instructor-led face-to-face (or online) 1 or 2 full day sessions	Understand the site Information Architecture Be comfortable and capable of managing permissions Understand the Governance Guide Understand the Design Document Know about any SharePoint customizations	Site Administrators	Prior to go-live
Quick Reference Guide (See **Quick Reference**)	Reference document May be printed and posted on cubicle walls	Understand how to access portal Understand a few basic and critically important aspects of the portal Have a reference document for metadata	All staff	At go-live
Portal Overview for All Staff (See **Go-Live Webinar**)	1-hour webinar Recorded and linked on the home page for new users	Familiar with key aspects of the portal Know how to navigate Know how to search Know where to get help Know where to make suggestions for change Feel comfortable (even excited) about the new portal	All users	Launch day or the day before Deliver several times to capture all users Record for on-demand viewing

See the documents referenced above at **https://lightlever.sharepoint.com/sites/book1**.

Timing

Time any training to align as closely as possible to when people will need the knowledge provided. For all-staff training, this is delivered just before go-live. With this approach we try to deliver the needed information such that the users can apply it right away. This way the training is more relevant and more effective.

One of my best coordinated training experiences was when I helped roll out a new Microsoft Office system for a client. I developed a half-day training program, and the client scheduled cohorts of 12 people to attend. While those 12 people were in the training room learning Office, the IT staff were at their workstations installing it. Users left their old system to get training on the new system, and when they returned to their desks they had that new system. We also arranged post-training deskside support—walking around the office, making sure no one had lingering questions as they settled in. This was a very effective training method. Rolling out a portal won't require the IT staff to install anything on the computers, but this is a good example of a coordinated effort for effective training, timed to coincide as closely as possible with system roll-out.

Lastly, when talking about timing, let's mention "anytime." The timing of on-demand video is "when I need it," and that is powerful. So use video extensively.

Training by Audience

Let's talk about *who* needs *what* training.

End Users

The end users—people using the portal daily—are your largest group, which means that training can be unwieldy and expensive. Remember that 80% of the users will accept change, 10% will be eager and about 10% will resist no matter what. Focus on the 80% you can and need to influence.

> **TEMPLATE:** Go-Live Webinar
>
> **Purpose:** to provide all staff introductory training and an initial overview of the intranet. To give a "good feeling" about the intranet.
>
> **Audience:** All staff
>
> Download templates at
> **https://lightlever.sharepoint.com/sites/book1**

It is not usually practical or cost-effective to do hands-on, face-to-face training for all users, so end-user training is delivered via webcast and recorded for future reference. Make sure you have a help page where people can easily find recorded videos. (When rolling out an Office 365 portal, I prefer to deliver training via Skype for Business. This has the side benefit of giving people more experience with Skype, which is a tool they already own.)

This group needs general knowledge about the portal, how to get around, and how to get on with their day-to-day work. And they need to feel good about this "big scary new system." Remember, change is hard for people. Focus on *user acceptance* just as much as you focus on *how-to*. Make sure you give them information about where to get more help—including promoting the Content Stewards, the suggestion box, help materials, and support videos.

Content Stewards

Oh yes, our beloved Content Stewards! This group needs a good overall understanding of the portal—not just how to use it, but deeper knowledge. Remember, Content Stewards support others, so consider this to be *power-users'* training with a *train-the-trainer* point of view.

Content Stewards need some of the same knowledge as the site administrators, so reuse materials where you can. Focus the Content Stewards on end-user functions with a solid foundation in SharePoint fundamentals, so they can feel confident to share that information with others. For example, they need to understand permissions policies (in the Governance Guide), and they should also understand how permissions are set and managed. Take the extra time to teach how to teach, "This is how permissions work, *and see how I am explaining it to you ... use these words and pictures to explain it others.*"

TEMPLATE: Content Stewards Training 1

TEMPLATE: Content Stewards Training 2

Purpose: to provide the structure and visuals for live hands-on training for Content Stewards. (Delivered in 2 half-day sessions.)

Audience: Content Stewards, Site Administrators, Trainers

Download the presentations at **https://lightlever.sharepoint. com/sites/book1**

Content Stewards must be placed in the workforce as "power users": they need to be able to do all the things that the end-users do, they need to do them well, *and they need to teach and support others*. To be clear, Content Stewards need an extra level of confidence in their ability to use the portal, and a deeper understanding. Deliver these sessions "hands-on" if possible.

And don't rush it. Often, we try to shorten training sessions to please busy users and cost-conscious managers. Stand your ground to make sure enough time is allocated to do the job well. Rushed training with limited time for discussion and review is frustrating for everyone.

In terms of ongoing training, in Content Stewards meetings (approximately monthly; see **Chapter 8** on page 77), make a training a regular agenda item. These sessions become a forum and a drumbeat of support where Content Stewards can bring questions, get answers, and educate each other. The meetings should become a Community of Practice where training is not just one-way (instructor to student) but is also collaborative, where any Content Steward bring a question on a technical issue, process, or governance, and one of their colleagues might answer it. Or they might bring some experience to share with the group: *"Bob asked me how to connect a network drive to the SharePoint library. We figured it out and it looks useful for others to know. This is how you do it."*

The Content Stewards are the linchpin to the success of your company portal; make sure they feel good about it, and they will spread that goodwill as they support the people around them.

Site Administrators

The organization should designate one to three people as SharePoint Site Administrators responsible for managing and maintaining the portal. These are generally Information Systems (IS or IT) staff. (If you're not sure who these are, raise the need for this ongoing support function with the Steering Committee. It needs to be filled.) This group will get one or two days of custom training to help them to support and maintain the portal.

In planning what to teach Site Administrators, recognize some limitations. The technology people will want to know all the cool details of

SharePoint, but you must remain focused and limit topics or the training becomes too unwieldy. If you have eager learners wanting to know "everything about SharePoint," direct them to a standard SharePoint Administrators course at a local training company, which will give them a solid foundation in all-things-SharePoint. You could make that course a prerequisite to your custom training. Your offering here, as part of the portal development project, is not general SharePoint training. Instead, focus on what's special and unique about their SharePoint instance and their portal. Teach as much of the important unique information as you can, without expecting the administrator training to be perfect or all-encompassing. Then make sure that you are available to answer questions and resolve issues.

Site Administrators should also have a good understanding of the governance rules, key lists, and libraries, permission structures and roles, group naming conventions, and information architecture. And they need specific directions, including how to add users to permissions groups, how to edit wiki pages, and how content approval works. Don't just teach the administrators the technical pieces—teach the process around them as well.

Administrator training is best done hands-on—where each person has their own computer—in small groups. Due to the technical topics, I recommend face-to-face classroom training, but if online is easier to schedule or less costly, it can also work. Yes, it is more convenient and easier to schedule training to use Skype for Business® or another web conferencing platform, but being in a room together will always get better engagement and better learning outcomes.

> **TEMPLATE:**
> **SharePoint Site Administrator Training**
>
> **Purpose:** to provide the structure and some visuals during a hands-on training for Site Administrators
>
> **Audience:** Sharepoint Administrators, Trainers
>
> Download the training at
> **https://lightlever.sharepoint.com/sites/book1**

The duration of the site administrator training will vary depending on the group's size, their experience level, and the complexity of the portal. Plan at least one full day and likely two days. To keep the learning effective, break training sessions into

3-hour modules, delivered over several days. Say 9:00 to noon on Monday, Wednesday, and Thursday. Plan a few 15-minute breaks to break up the morning and the afternoon.

Management and Executive Team

Don't forget the executive. As discussed in the chapter on User Engagement, the executive is an important group to nurture and involve. Typically, this cohort is very busy (and expensive), so they have little time or patience to sit down for training. Get creative and be efficient. Offer them a *portal overview* or *project update*, and don't call it "training." Carve out as much time as you can. You may be able to schedule a dedicated session, but more likely you will piggyback on an upcoming management meeting or executive retreat. In these situations, your target audience is already assembled, which is 80% of the challenge of getting in front of this group. You may only be able to get their attention for a half-hour or less, but do whatever you can to give the executive an overview and promote the portal. The **Executive Overview Presentation** in **Chapter 6** (page 59) can be adapted for this purpose.

Prepare a very concise PowerPoint to guide your presentation. Offer the PowerPoint to be included in the minutes and develop it with that in mind. As mentioned, this presentation can be disguised as a *project update* and will include information on the structure and function of the portal. If you have time to demonstrate the system live, consider this opportunity carefully. It is easy to fall down a rabbit hole during a live presentation, as people ask questions and, being eager to please, you go off on a tangent and are distracted from your core messages and planned agenda. Stay focused, keep it very tight, showing a few important topics. It is much better to show three topics very clearly and thoroughly than it is to show 10 topics quickly that confuse your audience. Stick to the home page and a high-level glance at features the executive might use, such as documents, calendars, and contact lists.

Plan Q&A time and have a strategy for what to do with questions that might take too long to answer. For example, *"That's a great question that will take a bit more time to answer. Can I stop by later this week to show you that?"*

Develop allies on the executive team that can coach you (e.g., from the Steering Committee and/or your Project Sponsor). Ask for that coaching, and ask them to support you during the presentation. Whereas it may be politically unwise for you to brush off the CEO's question about offline document libraries, a member of the executive is in a better position to say, "*let's look at this in a future session*" or "*we would like to come to your office to give you and your staff desk-side training and support. There we can answer all your questions and make sure you have what you need.*"

It is immensely valuable and highly beneficial to the success of your portal to get top management interested and engaged. And remember, there is always a thread of *promotion* running through all these meetings. Be highly prepared and clearly organized, stay enthusiastic, talk about business benefits, and you'll be on the road to getting this important group on board.

Training Methods

Different methods of training have advantages and disadvantages. Consider, for example, the trade-off between the time it takes to develop a course and the time it takes to deliver. If you plan a video training or an e-learning course, it takes more development effort than a face-to-face course, but then it's fundamentally free to deliver. That said, nothing beats face-to-face training to connect and support people. So even though face-to-face is the most expensive method to execute, it should always be your first choice.

Also consider if you should be using hands-on, as opposed to presentation-style, training. It is much easier to manage a training session where you just demonstrate features, without user exercises, but the tradeoff is significant. If you really need your trainees to learn the materials well, organize a room full of computers (or ask people to bring their own), and schedule the training with enough time that people get to *do* as well as *see*. According to Confucius, "*I hear, and I forget. I see, and I remember. I do, and I understand.*"

Knowledge Transfer through Development

Some training is accomplished "organically" throughout the project while working with the Design Team, Migration Team, and Steering Committee. By being directly involved in the decision-making process and through "micro-trainings" that come up in meetings, these people will be familiar with the new portal by the time it rolls out and will have a varying degree of confidence and capability. This is discussed in depth in **Chapter 3** (page 17).

Formal Classroom Training

Sometimes a formal, structured SharePoint classroom training course from a good training company is what advanced users need. Many training schools and online training classes are available. This training is necessarily generic (not customized to your portal). The downside of generic training is because it is general, people can't connect the learning to their system. The up side is that it is less expensive and ready to go, as it has already been developed for a mass market.

Search for local training schools or online resources like lynda.com and YouTube.com and use these to supplement, not replace, your custom training.

Support Videos

Support videos or training snippets are a very effective, and practical training tool. Video can be watch as required, on demand, so is an excellent learning aid and effective support tool.

Design and record a set of 5-10 minute support videos that provide portal overview and "how to" clips. Use a screen capture software (I use SnagIt[7]) with a headset to capture good quality voiceover. Call these "Support Videos" rather than "Training Videos" to present them as informal and task-focused as opposed to formal training with lesson plans and learning objectives. These videos are designed to train and assist people with a just-in-time-delivery model. The audience is primarily

---

7   SnagIt   software   is   available   here: **https://www.techsmith.com/screen-capture.html**. I have no affiliation with Techmith or any subsidiaries. SnagIt is no longer free to use, but I find it is money well spent!

end-users, but you may use this same format to create advanced topics for Content Stewards and Site Administrators as well.

Support Video topics usually include:

- Site overview including navigation;
- Browser tips and tricks, including browser standards; book-marks, home pages;
- Working with documents, including versions and sharing;
- Working with the Contact list, including connect to Outlook;
- Working with the Calendar, including connect to Outlook;
- The fundamentals of Search;
- Updating your User Profile;
- All about metadata.

AND MAY ALSO INCLUDE:

- How to edit wiki pages;
- Permissions overview;
- How to manage permissions;
- How to create and modify Views;
- Using Managed Metadata;
- Etc.

Go-Live Webinar

Plan a 45- to 60-minute webinar to coincide with the portal launch. This will show all users key portal components, where to find and use them, and some basic "how-to." This "all users webinar" or "go-live webinar" shows the new system in action at a high level. And, as always, this webinar is designed to generate excitement and positivity around the new portal.

TEMPLATE: Go-Live Webinar

Purpose: To provide a site overview, and gentle introduction to their new portal.

Audience: All Staff and contractors

Download the webinar at **https://lightlever.sharepoint.com/sites/book1**

Deliver this training as close to possible to the go-live date. For example, if the portal will be live on Monday morning, the first thing the staff will do Monday morning is attend the go-live webinar.

This webinar is another place for your promotional skills to shine: Think about the "what's in it for me" attitude that people always have and stay consistently enthusiastic. It is important that the users feel your excitement as you explain, *Look at this new portal and see how it's going to save you time and help you work better together*" (referring to the portal purpose statement and stated business problems, of course).

An important topic in the all-user webinar is "how to get more help." Direct users to the help page and support videos, and ensure they understand the support structure, including the Content Stewards, the suggestion box, and the role of the help desk.

Emphasize that this new system was designed and developed by a representative group of their peers (the Design Team), and we have done our best to design it to serve them well. It will take a little time and effort to know how to use it, we will help them achieve that mastery. And assure them that the portal will evolve over time based on their needs and feedback.

Brown Bag Sessions

For ongoing training and engagement, consider regularly scheduled user-group meetings, sometimes called Brown Bag sessions. These should be monthly sessions, usually occurring over the noon hour where people bring their own lunch, or lunch is provided. You may call these *Community of Practice* or *SharePoint User Group* meetings and shed the "Brown Bag" moniker and lunch timing. These sessions create a rhythm of training and support for all users. Everyone is invited to attend, and we ask them to contribute topics and questions before, during, and after the sessions.

You as the facilitator will have several topics to present. Session topics may be similar to the support videos listed above, and also should include success stories, best practices, or planned new features.

Invite anyone, especially Content Stewards, to present tips, tricks, and user success stories. This is "everyone's portal," so give everyone an opportunity to speak and create a sense of collaboration and shared ownership. Nothing beats seeing your peers using the portal well and demonstrating how they're *actually* solving business problems.

Getting guest presenters to commit to speak, even for five minutes, can be challenging. Be prepared to encourage, remind, support, cajole ... and maybe even bribe with a prize or a free lunch. The Content Stewards are one of your prime sources for presenters, so they especially should be encouraged to take turns stepping up. Consider adding these presentations to the Content Stewards role description.

PART 2

SharePoint in Practice

Practical Business Solutions

Introduction to Part 2

This part of *SharePoint in Practice* provides specifications for some common business problems, solved with SharePoint. They are presented in our Design Document format (see **Chapter 3** on page 17 for details).

Working examples, and in some cases, downloads, are available at our Office 365 companion site.

> To access on-line content, log in into the Office 365 companion site.
>
> **Site:** https://sharepointinpractice.com/resources/#part2
>
> **Login:** reader@sharepointinpractice.com
>
> **Password:** Pr@ctic@l!
>
> Please don't share this login information.

Suggestion Box

⟡ **See the Suggestion Box live on the *SharePoint in Practice* site (https://lightlever.sharepoint.com/sites/book1/Lists/suggest).**

Business Problem

How do we gather guidance and direction from the user community? How do we allow our beloved users to easily post suggestions and ideas? How do we manage and respond in an efficient manner?

Practical Solution

Most portals that Lightlever has built include a suggestion box. A successful company portal is *for the people and by the people*, and the suggestion box helps collect the thoughts and views of those people. In its simplest form, this is a vanilla SharePoint discussion board. You may add some custom fields to the board (see below), but that's not strictly necessary. In the model described here, a custom list was used, and as this is the more interesting solution, it is included here.

The suggestion box is linked to the help page and the top menu, and is often surfaced on the home page as a list of Frequently Asked Questions or Recent Suggestions. During the Go-Live presentations and all end-user trainings, you invite people to use the suggestion box to provide ideas and feedback. In fact, whenever you have the opportunity, encourage users to post their questions and desired improvements in "their" suggestion box.

Be careful to not allow suggestions to stagnate in the suggestion box. Create an alert mechanism so you can respond in a timely manner. This could be a simple SharePoint Alert for you, for the Content Stewards Chair, or for all Content Stewards. You can also tailor those alerts with a SharePoint workflow.

However you do it, make sure your portal has a suggestion box feature, and that people use it.

SharePoint in Practice Design: Suggestion Box

Suggestion Box List

Web Address: */suggest*

SharePoint Description: *Use this to submit suggestions or ideas to improve the portal, or from a general business point of view. You may submit anonymously.*

This custom list is designed with simple fields to capture a suggestion and uses a workflow move it to the list of live suggestions and, if desired, anonymize the posted suggestion.

Metadata

Metadata Field	Data Type	Mandatory?	Default	Description
Suggestion Summary	Single line of text	Yes	None	The suggestion or question to be answered (title field).
Suggestion Type	Choice of • Accounting • Computer Systems • Customer Service • Human Resources • Portal • General	Yes	General	What type of question or suggestion is this? This may drive who gets to answer.
Details	Multiple lines of text	No	Blank	Provide as much detail as you can for this suggestion, including web links and images.
Post Anonymously?	Choice of • No • Yes	Yes	No	Should this item be "anonymized" to hide the identity of the person who posted?

Views

- All Suggestions

Suggestions and FAQs List

Web Address: /suggestions

SharePoint Description: *This lists suggestions and questions (which may be anonymous) and their responses. You can also search for previously posted questions and their answers.*

This custom list is normally populated by a SharePoint Workflow triggered on the Suggestion Box List. This is done to anonymize the suggestion, and to simplify the entry form. SharePoint *Content Approval* will be used to ensure only designated responders can answer. A permissions group of *Suggestion-Responders* will be created to manage this. Alerts will be set up to immediately alert responders of new questions posted.

The intention of this list is that people can search the list first, and if the answer they seek is not there, they can post a question. Questions will be answered within one work day to validate the tool and ensure people have the information they need to do their jobs effectively.

Metadata

Metadata Field	Data Type	Mandatory?	Default	Description
Suggestion Summary	Single line of text	Yes	None	The suggestion or question to be answered (title field).
Suggestion Type	Choice of • Accounting • Computer Systems • Customer Service • Human Resources • Portal • General	Yes	General	What type of question or suggestion is this? This may drive who gets to answer.

Metadata Field	Data Type	Mandatory?	Default	Description
Details	Multiple lines of text	No	Blank	Provide as much detail as you can for this suggestion, including web links and images.
Submitted By	User	No	Anonymous	If not anonymous, then who submitted the suggestion?
Status	Choice of • New • Under Review • Answered • FAQ	Yes	New	Used in Views to filter questions. If a question has been read, but the answer will take more time, the status is set to "Under Review."
Response	Multiple lines of text	No	Blank	The official response to the suggestion or question.
Response By	Single line of text	No	Anonymous	Who provided the response to the question?

Views

- Answered Questions (default)
- All Questions
- Active Questions, grouped by Type
- FAQs: all questions where status is FAQ

Workflow: Anonymize Suggestion

The following workflow fires when new items are created in the Suggestion Box list, and to create items in the *Suggestions and FAQs* list, stripping out user information to create anonymous posts as required. The workflow should be published under a generic "Workflow Manager" SharePoint login, not a named person, since the impersonation step runs as the person who *published* the workflow.

Workflow Set-Up

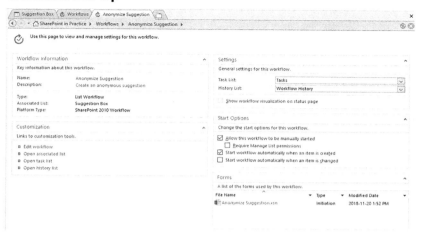

Workflow Steps

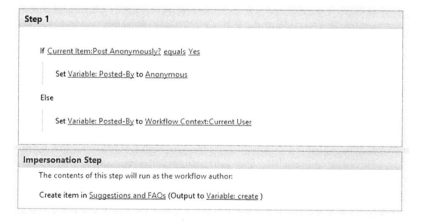

Create Item Action Details

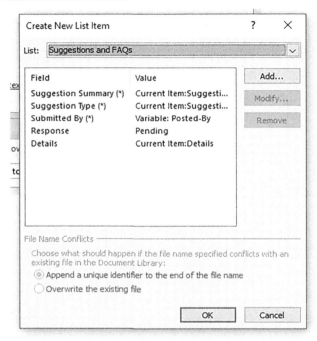

Ideas for Enhancement

- Use a discussion board to leverage simple out-of-the-box functionality for threaded discussion. Note that the custom list
  solution (shown) provides greater control over views. Discussion boards have a lot of baked-in capability but less flexibility
  with fields and views.

- Use PowerApps, JavaScript, or InfoPath to simplify and beautify the entry form.

- Use Content Types to drive the anonymization, rather than
  managing two separate lists.

- Add functionality to send posted suggestions to different
  groups based on user-selected categories. You can do this with
  a helper list (e.g., Suggestion Box Managers) that is used as a

look-up in the workflow. The SharePoint workflow is used to trigger an email to the manager, based on the category chosen.

- Add functionality to automatically email the person who posted the suggestions, when updated or marked "answered." Again, this is done with a SharePoint workflow.

Governance Notes

- Who is responsible for responding to suggestions? What is their stated/committed time frame to respond? What is the alert mechanism? Is a reminder mechanism in place?

- What's the process for follow-up with the person who posted the suggestion?

- When do old suggestions get deleted? An annual purge? Manual or automatic?

- If you are using this list as an FAQ, who is responsible to tag answered suggestions as Frequently Asked? Where are they displayed—home page, help page, other?

Timesheet

❖ **See the Timesheet live and download the timesheet report Excel spreadsheet at the *Sharepoint in Practice* site (https:// lightlever.sharepoint.com/sites/book1/Lists/Timesheet).**

Business Problem

How can we track staff time worked for invoicing, reporting, and future reference? This is especially useful for consulting firms, for billing time against projects, and in any situation where people are required to track their hours. How do we set up time tracking in a way that is easy to enter, and easy for administration staff or management to use for reporting and invoicing?

Practical Solution

Our example timesheet is a custom SharePoint list with fields for who worked, on what, when, and for how long.

The entry form can be simple or enhanced, and an Excel workbook can be attached for advanced reporting: using Export to Excel, we connect an Excel data query to the list, which is easily refreshed to provide pivot table reporting on current timesheet data.

SharePoint in Practice Design: Timesheet

Timesheet List

Web Address: */timesheet*

SharePoint Description: *Tracks who worked on what, when. It is used for accounting and billing purposes.*

Metadata

Metadata Field	Data Type	Mandatory?	Default	Description
Work Date	Date	Yes	TODAY	When was the work performed?
Work Done By	Choice or User look-up	Yes	The person cur-rently logged in	Who did the work?
Project or Job	Choice field or Look-up against a list of projects	Yes	None	
Hours	Number	Yes	None	How many hours were worked?
Details	Multiple lines of text	No	None	What are the details of the work per-formed?
Status	Choice of • New • Processed	Yes	New	Used by adminis-trators to manage timesheet records.
Internal Comments	Single line of text (Rename TITLE field)	No	None	Comments not seen by the client.

Views

- *My Work This Week* (default): filter by the current user, and group by date, sort in descending order (recent first). Show totals

- *Unprocessed Records:* all users, filter by Status *not equal to* Processed

- *All Items:* all items, all fields, used for management and main-tenance

Ideas for Enhancement

- Add other fields as needed for management or reporting: time category, client name, GL codes, billable y/n, etc.

- Devise an export/import capability to load timesheet data into your accounting program (e.g. QuickBooks, Quicken, or Simply Accounting).

- Improve input methods: Use PowerApps, InfoPath, or other form development tools to simplify or beautify input and edit forms. For example, the input form could hide the name field, and make it default to the current user. This creates a simpler interface and forces the user to only enter information for themselves.

- Improve archive methods: Create a workflow or other process to automatically move old records to cold storage.

- Include a Quick Edit view for entry. If people are familiar with this "datasheet view" it can be very useful.

- Add functionality to default as many fields as possible, including name, date, and with some extra work, Project.

Governance Notes

- If you have a large staff and especially if you are tracking detailed time sheets per employee, per project, you will accumulate many timesheet records. SharePoint won't display more than 5,000 records in a view, so it is important to stay on top of your data and archive it on a regular basis. Most of my clients use their timesheets on a monthly basis for invoicing and reconciliation against their accounting program. They archive items on a quarterly basis, so they have the current quarter available and the previous quarter saved but removed from the timesheet list.

- If you are using a look-up on a SharePoint Projects list (against which time is tracked), keep that list up to date by removing old records.

- Be sure to train people on how to use this tool. Otherwise, they may not use it properly and could end up creating a lot more work for you (as the administrator) and for your accounting staff.

Policy Manual with Index

✪ **See the Policy Manual live on the *SharePoint in Practice* site (https://lightlever.sharepoint.com/sites/book1/policies).**

Business Problem

How can we present a large and complex manual or set of documents in a way that it easily navigable and maintainable? How can we convert a large document into wiki pages so it is easy to read and manage in SharePoint?

Practical Solution

Converting a large historical document (like an employee handbook) or set of documents (like policy a manual or standard operating procedures) to a wiki can be very rewarding. If your team or client is reluctant to convert, or has trouble understanding the benefits of wiki-vs-Word, emphasize the online nature of the wiki. Wiki pages are accessible by the web browser, so no application, such as Word or Adobe Acrobat, needs to open. Also, wiki pages easily link to other objects in your site (using [[link|display]] format), and SharePoint will manage those links if they change. Not so in Word or PDF. **Here is a video** that describes what's the same and what's different: **https://www.youtube.com/watch?v=n84kRMDLV8Q.**

In this application, you are starting with a large Word document or set of documents. These will be organized into sections and may have images and tables. For simplicity, we will call it a Policy Manual, but it could be any large document or set of documents.

How to convert a Word file to a set of Wiki pages:

1. Create a Wiki library with metadata (see below). Alternatively, customize the SitePages library to integrate cleanly with the set of home pages.

2. Create a new Page. We'll call it "Policy Manual Home."

3. Create an index on that page, one link per section. Watch this video for a how-to: **https://www.youtube.com/watch?v=XlM8TJvTqI4**.

4. For each section:

   ▪ In Word, save any images as individual files (png or jpg), using right-click *Save as Picture…* .

   ▪ Copy the entire section from Word.

   ▪ Click on the wiki index to create a new page.

   ▪ Paste in the copied content.

   ▪ Save the page to avoid losing your work.

   ▪ Edit the page to insert the images you saved previously— they will not have pasted successfully.

   ▪ Check and clean up formatting, especially tables.

   ▪ Create [[Home|Return to Home]] link on each page.

To enhance your manual, include an index like the one below, Add metadata to generate the index, which of course is just a Grouped view.

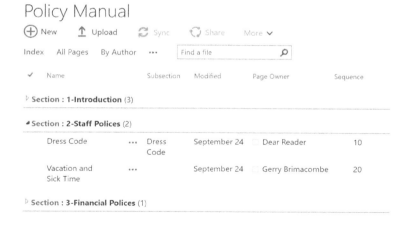

SharePoint in Practice Design: Policy Manual

Policy Manual Wiki

Web Address: */policies or /SitePages*

SharePoint Description: *This wiki library contains and categorizes policies, procedures, and guidelines.*

This wiki library has custom fields and views to generate an index. It has unique permissions to limit who can edit and read the Policy Manual.

Metadata

Metadata Field	Data Type	Mandatory?	Default	Description
Section	Choice: 1. Introduction 2. Staff Policies 3. Financial Policies 4. Health and Safety Etc.	Yes	None	Which major section does this page fall under? Note: The prefix numbers help you manage the index and sort order.
Subsection	Single line of text	No	None	Within the section, is this page further categorized? (This could also be a look-up field, but only if subsections are standardized.)
Sequence	Number	No	50	A sequence or "sort order" number that can be used in views to control the order in which pages are displayed (if other than alphabetical is desired).

Metadata Field	Data Type	Mandatory?	Default	Description
Page Owner	User name	Yes	None	Who is responsible for this page? One person only.
Page Review Date	Date	No	[Today] +183 (creation date + 6 months)	Designates when this page should be reviewed and possibly deleted or archived. Drives a view that shows files to be reviewed.
Notes	Single line of text	No	None	Brief note about this page, including update status, etc.

Views

The following Views will be developed for this wiki library:

- *Index View* – group pages by Section, and by Subsection

- *All Pages* – default view with all metadata shown, in folders

- *Recent Pages* – all Pages shown without folders, sorted descending by modified date

- *Group by Owner* – grouping by Page Owner, without folders

- *For Review* – showing pages in which the "Review Date" is passed or within 30 days ([Page Review Date]<[Today]+30)

Ideas for Enhancement

- Include a reminder workflow to email Page Owners when their pages are up for review.

- Include a "search this policy manual" capability.

- Add a policies and procedures custom search page.

- Support printing of selected sections.

- Add metadata and views to categorize by Page Type (Policy, Procedure, Guideline, etc.).

- Create a standard wiki page template that standardizes layouts, including core navigation and header/footer. The easiest way to do this is to create a wiki page to be used as a template, and create a Site Workflow that copies that template page to create a new one.

- If permissions or pages are managed by a department or business area, consider sub-folders to group the pages and manage permissions. Then use "without folders" in most of your views.

- Create a helper list to make the Sections and Subsections into look-up fields and therefore standardized.

Governance Notes

- Create a standard wiki page layout for ease of navigation. This may be driven by a template as described above or may just be a set of documented standards in the Governance Guide.

- Keep pages up to date. Use a reminder or alert, manual or automated to ask Page Owners to check and/or update their page.

- Consider who can edit pages. Of course, this is a wiki library, so permissions are manageable. You may want to use Content Approval to allow anyone to edit, and allow only a small group to approve changes.

Leave Calendar

✥ **See the** Leave Calendar **live on the** *SharePoint in Practice* **site** **(https://lightlever.sharepoint.com/sites/book1/Lists/leavecal/).**

Business Problem

How can I easily view and track "who is where"? How do I check when people are on vacation? Can we use SharePoint to review and approve staff requests for vacation or leave?

Practical Solution

The leave calendar is a common tool used to track and, if desired, *approve* leave time. In its simplest form, this is a SharePoint calendar that has an additional field showing *who is away*. The calendar can be customized to categorize each entry by type of leave (e.g. holiday, illness, leave of absence, parental leave, conference, training, etc.).

A slightly enhanced version of the leave calendar adds a leave *approval* mechanism using standard SharePoint *content approval*. This way an employee can enter a leave "request" in the calendar, and thanks to content approval, only users with list management permissions can see the leave request until it's approved. We recommend coupling this approach with SharePoint Alerts so that managers know when a new leave request is created. Managers are then able to open the calendar, look at the request in the context of the entire calendar, and approve or decline.

The set-up for content approval is very simple. See below and read this article for more information: **https://tinyurl.com/ContentApproval**.

1. In Calendar Settings, *Versioning Settings, Require content approval for submitted items?*, select "YES"

Settings ‣ Versioning Settings

Content Approval

Specify whether new items or changes to existing items should remain in a
draft state until they have been approved.   Learn about requiring approval.

Require content approval for
submitted items?

  Yes   ● No

2. Set permissions to give all managers who need to be
    able to approve leave "list management rights" on the
    calendar list.

SharePoint in Practice Design: Leave Calendar

Leave Calendar List

Web Address: */leavecal*

SharePoint Description: *Calendar to track "who is away when" at a high-level.*

All staff are able to enter leave events into this calendar. Content Approval is enabled so managers can approve events as entered or reject, asking for changes.

Metadata

Standard Calendar columns, plus the following.

Metadata Field	Data Type	Mandatory?	Default	Description
Who's Away	Person (not group)	Yes	None	Who is the person taking leave?

Metadata Field	Data Type	Mandatory?	Default	Description
Event Type	Choice of • Confer-ence • Earned Time Off • Medical Holiday • Training • z Other	Yes	Blank	Could rename and reuse the *Category* field if you wish

Views

- *All Events Calendar View by Week:* Show *Who's Away* and the event *Title* in the Week View.

▣ Calendar Columns

Specify columns to be represented in the Calendar Views. The Title fields are required fields. The Sub Heading fields are optional fields.

Month View Title:
[Who's Away ▾]

Week View Title:
[Who's Away ▾]

Week View Sub Heading:
[Title ▾]

Day View Title:
[Who's Away ▾]

Day View Sub Heading:
[Title ▾]

▣ Default Scope

Choose the default scope for the view.

Default scope:
- ○ Day
- ◉ Week
- ○ Month

You can change this at any time while using the calendar.

- *View by Type*
  - Conference and Training
  - Holidays
  - All Events
- *Overlay View:* Show the above views in the same calendar, color-coded

Ideas for Enhancement

- The next level of complexity is to build some more logic for streamlining approvals. You can use workflow, so when an employee requests, we look up their **approving manager** from a contact list or from Active Directory. We can then email the contact person for approval. This email could include hyperlinks or buttons to *approve* or *decline* the leave request.

- Use PowerApps, InfoPath, or another form tool to clean up the input form to simplify entry and look more professional.

- Use a third-party tool or JavaScript to make calendar color-coding (based on leave type) work better than the out-of-the-box Calendar Overlay tool, which is quite limited.

- Use calendar overlays to visually distinguish between *pending* and *approved* leave items.

- Create a workflow that changes the permissions of each item so only the manager and the employee requesting leave can edit the item.

Governance Notes

- Can accounting or HR use this list to track actual vacation days used per employee? (Yes, if it is managed well.)

- When do you delete old content—annually? What is the process? Is this manual, or is there an automated (or semi-automated) tool required?

- Be aware of permissions: If you don't want people seeing where others are, then consider the permissions of each item be set (by workflow).

- Make sure it is clear to everyone what this calendar is used for. It is for tracking when people are away, not for meetings, other events, or personal details.

Board Portal

❖ See the Board Portal **live on the** *SharePoint in Practice* **site**
(https://lightlever.sharepoint.com/sites/book1/board-portal).

Business Problem

How can we efficiently share important, and potentially confidential, materials with the Board of Directors? Board and committee members are busy people, often external to an organization. They work off-site and may be challenged by technology, and this board is seldom their only job. They do not want to wade through unnecessary content—they want to go straight to what's relevant to them.

Practical Solution

The goal is to create a SharePoint site that directors can use to easily access board materials. The board portal can be complex, but of course we will keep it as simple as possible. On its basic level, the Board Portal comprises a calendar and a document library. The calendar is used to schedule board and committee meetings, and the document library is linked from the calendar to show all files relating to the meeting. A unique meeting number, or meeting ID, is used to link these lists.

SharePoint in Practice Design: Board Portal

Meeting Calendar List

Web Address: */meetings*

SharePoint Description: *Calendar to track Board and Committee meetings*

This is a standard SharePoint calendar with some customization as detailed below. The calendar part is placed top and center on the Board Portal. All board members are set up with SharePoint Alerts so they are immediately informed of any changes.

Metadata

Metadata Field	Data Type	Manda-tory?	Default	Description
Meeting Code	Single line of text	Yes	None	Could be entered by the user creating the item or generated by workflow.
Meeting Type	Choice of • Standard Meeting • In Camera • Public • Finance Committee • Governance Committee • Extraordinary Meeting • Members Meeting (e.g. AGM)	Yes	Stan-dard Meeting	What type of meeting is this? Can be used for filters and views.
Link to Documents	Hyperlink	No	None	A link to a view showing all documents for this meeting.

Views

- Standard Calendar views
- Meeting by Committee: Group by Meeting Type
- Upcoming meetings: based on current events view

Meeting Documents Library

Web Address: */docs*

SharePoint Description: *All documents relevant to this board*

This is the main document library for the board. We have one document library to store all documents in one spot and apply permissions as required to restrict who can view what.

Metadata

Metadata Field	Data Type	Manda-tory?	Default	Description
Meeting Code	Look-up on *Meeting Cal-endar*	No	None	Look-up against the Meeting cal-endar answers the question, "which meeting does this document relate to?"
Document Owner	Person (user look-up)	Yes	None	Who is respon-sible for this document?
Document Type	Choice of • Minutes • Board Pack-ages • Presentations	No	None	Classify the docu-ments if needed.
Comment	Single line of text	No	None	Optional free text description of the file.

Views

- All Documents: showing folders (based on permissions)
- "20 most recently changed" without folders
- Documents Grouped by Owner (ignore folders)
- Documents Grouped by meeting type (ignore folders)
- Documents Grouped by meeting code (ignore folders)

Actions and Motions (Meeting Outcomes List)

Web Address: */actions*

SharePoint Description: *This list tracks Board actions, motions, and minutes, including their current status*

Using Content Approval, new items entered have "draft status" until approved by the board secretary.

Metadata

This list is based on a SharePoint task list, with the following modifications.

Metadata Field	Data Type	Manda-tory?	Default	Description
Meeting Code	Look-up on *Meeting Calendar*	No	None	Look-up against the Meeting calendar, answers the question, "Which meeting does this item relate to?"
Record Type	Choice: • Action • Motion • Minute	Yes	Action	Use to classify and group items
Notes	Multiple lines of text	No	Blank	If needed, include comments, including reference to the Agenda item being discussed.

Views

- All Items
- My items
- Overdue items
- Open Items: items that have a status not "Completed" and not "Cancelled"

Ideas for Enhancement

- Often our board portal will include a contact list. The list includes details and roles for all board members and support staff. The contact list can include metadata and views to filter by committee membership, so it is easy to see who does what.

- Simplify this site to bare basics to reduce any distraction or clutter for the users.

- Create a custom list to manage Agendas and allow people to post and build agendas collaboratively.

- Create a custom web part page that allows the user to select a Meeting Code or Meeting Type and see all pertinent documents and actions on one page. This may be done with web part filter connections.

Governance Notes

- Governing a board portal requires quite a bit of attention. Board members are not always comfortable with technology and will have no tolerance for error or confusion. The portal must be kept up-to-date and accurate if it is going to be used. For these reasons, there should be a Board Secretary or equivalent in charge of managing the site.

- Managing passwords becomes very important. With Office 365, we recommend giving Board Members external access so they don't have an additional password to track.

- Permissions are critical in the maintenance of a board portal. If the structure or members of the board change, one key governance task is to add and remove members. This is especially important to make sure access is not left in place for ex-Board Members. Managing permissions by *group* rather than individual makes this task easier.

- Consider a *conflict of interest* capability where the board secretary could flag various items, documents, meetings, or tasks with the user names of members who have a "conflict of interest" with this item. You can then set up a workflow to update permissions on individual items. SharePoint security trimming will hide those items from the conflicted users.

- Make sure that when you update the site, you make a point of documenting the changes, including permissions modifications.

A SharePoint "Shopping Cart"

✧ **See the** Shopping Cart **live on the *SharePoint in Practice* site (https://lightlever.sharepoint.com/sites/book1/shopcart), and download a** PowerPoint **presentation, the** JavaScript file, **and the** Order Now button **from the Site Assets Library (https:// lightlever.sharepoint.com/sites/book1/shopcart/SiteAsset/).**

Business Problem

How can we enable staff to be able to select from a list of supplies and receive shipments from head office? This needs to be easy for users to place orders, and for head office to manage fulfillment. It would be nice to have the ability to re-order since the same supplies are requested repeatedly. (No payment is attached to these transactions.)

Practical Solution

This is largely an out-of-the-box SharePoint solution that uses custom lists, views, workflow, and a little bit of JavaScript. Here is the high-level flow of the business process.

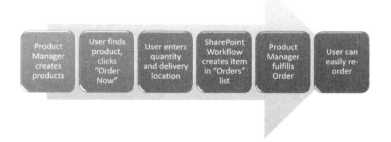

Three lists drive the shopping cart, all connected via look-up fields:

1. *Product Categories* is used as a look-up in the Product List to standardize product classification;

2. *Product* list creates an index of products and allows people to order; and

3. *Orders* list shows what is currently on order, and by whom.

A workflow is attached to the Product list to handle ordering. When started, it adds orders to the Orders list, and notifies the appropriate people to initiate fulfillment.

SharePoint in Practice Design: Shopping Cart

Shopping Cart Categories List

Web Address: */shopcat*

SharePoint Description: *This is a list of product categories for the Shopping Cart.*

This list is used as a look-up to classify and organize the Shopping Cart Products list.

Metadata

Metadata Field	Data Type	Mandatory?	Default	Description
Category	Single line of text	Yes		
Sub-Category	Single line of text	No		
Description	Multiple lines of text (rich text)	No	None	
Product Manager	User	Yes		Who manages orders in this category?
Category-lu	Calculated Single line of text =[Category] &"/"&[Sub-Category]	Yes		Used as the primary look-up field.

Views

- By Category: All products grouped by Category

Shopping Cart Products List

Web Address: */shopprod*

SharePoint Description: *This is a list of products that can be ordered.*

This list is readable by all staff and managed by Communications and Purchasing staff. To place an order, the user scrolls through the list, expanding Category groups as required, and clicks a button to start a workflow.

Metadata

Metadata Field	Data Type	Mandatory?	Default	Description
Product Code	Single line of text	No	None	A unique code
Product Name	Single line of text	Yes		
Description	Multiple lines of text (HTML)	No	None	
Category	Look-up on Categories (Category-lu list)	Yes	None	Used to create grouped index
Order Now	Single line of text	No		This field is overridden by the JavaScript to create the Order Now button

Views

- By Category: All products grouped by Category

Shopping Cart Orders

Web Address: */shopcart*

SharePoint Description: *This is a list of people's orders, as generated by the shopping cart.*

The shopping cart is a simple product ordering tool used by purchasing and communications to gather request for mailing supplies, communications materials, and the like. This list is used to capture and manage orders.

Metadata

This is a custom SharePoint list with columns as follows.

Metadata Field	Data Type	Mandatory?	Default	Description
Ordered By	User	Yes	None	Who ordered this product?
Order Status	Choice • New • Pending • Fulfilled • Canceled	Yes	New	
Product Name	Look-up on Products List	Yes	None	Which product is wanted?
Quantity	Integer	Yes	1	How many are required?
Product Manager	User	Yes	None	Who will fulfill this order?
Comments	Single line of text	No	None	Comments regarding this order (repurpose TITLE field)
Date Required	Date and Time	Yes	Today + 7	When is this order required?
Date Ordered	Date and Time	Yes	Today	When was this product ordered or reordered?

Views

- Current by Manager: All products grouped by Product Manager, filtered to exclude Fulfilled and Cancelled items

- My Current Orders: All products grouped by Ordered By, filtered to exclude Fulfilled and Cancelled items

- Order Management: datasheet view

- Reorder: show recent fulfilled orders for the current user

- All Items

Workflow: Order Product

This workflow is attached to the Products list and is used to order a product.

Initiation Parameters:

- Quantity

- Date Required

- Deliver to Branch

- Comments

Create new item in Shopping Cart Orders:

- Product Name: from Current Item

- Ordered By: Submitted By

- Quantity: from Workflow Parameter, default to 1 if blank

- Deliver to Branch: from Workflow Parameter

- Comments: from Workflow Parameter

- Date Required: from Workflow Parameter, Today + 7 if blank

- Product Manager: Look-up from Product Categories to find who is responsible for fulfilling this order

- Due Date: Date Required (default today + 7 days) from workflow parameter entered by user

- Order Date: Today

- Order Status: NEW

(We could generate an email in this workflow, but recommend the Product Manager use Alerts on Orders list instead, which is easier to manage and maintain.)

Create a Clickable Order Now Button

❖ **For more details on implementation, see** a PowerPoint **at https://lightlever.sharepoint.com/sites/book1.**

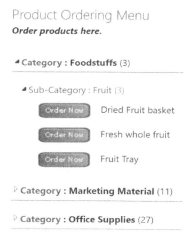

The Button that Starts a Workflow

1. Get or make a small "Order Now" graphic (approximately 72x22 pixels) or download the one pictured above from **https://lightlever.sharepoint.com/sites/book1.**

2. Upload to the Site Assets Library.

3. Copy the relative URL (for example, /SiteAssets/order_now.png) and save to a NotePad file, for later copy/paste into JavaScript.

JavaScript and JSLink

1. You will create a JavaScript file (see below):

   - JavaScript will override the *Order Now* field with some HTML;
   - The HTML displays a button;
   - The button launches the *Order Product* workflow.

2. On the page that will display the button:
   - Edit the Web part.
   - Make sure Order Now field is in view.
   - Add link to the JavaScript file in the JSLink field of the web part properties.

3. URLs for JavaScript
   - Use Relative URLs
     - We need the relative URL of the Button (/SiteAssets/order_now.png)
     - Paste into JavaScript as variable *sButtonImage*
   - We need the relative URL of the Workflow initiation page:
     - After the Workflow is ready (URL changes whenever the workflow is published or re-published)
     - Navigate to the Workflow start page
     - Copy the URL from the web browser address bar
   - We will copy two parts, before and after the ID= (e.g., ID=123). This is the unique ID that tells the Workflow which item to operate on.
   - Paste into JavaScript as variables *sWorkflowURLPart1* and *sWorkflowURLPart2*

4. Upload the JavaScript:
   - After editing as per above;
   - Upload to your Site Assets Library
   - Copy the file URL and paste into NotePad

5. On the SharePoint page that will display the [Order Now] button:
   - Edit the Product Orders web part;
   - Make sure *Order Now* field is in the view;
   - In the JSLink field of the web part properties, paste the link to your JavaScript file

JavaScript Function ShoppingCartButton.js

This JavaScript is downloadable from the *SharePoint in Practice* site, and included here for reference and clarity.

```
// Define a function that will run as a JS Link
// based on http://www.aerieconsulting.com/blog/using-a-js-link-override-in-
sharepoint-online


(function ( ) {

// Set up a field context, specifying the function that
// will change what is displayed for Order Now
     var oFldCtx = {};
     oFldCtx.Templates = {};

// Note that "Order_x0020_Now" is the name of the field where I will display
my image.
// The name must be the INTERNAl NAME.
// If you are not sure, one way to see the INTERNAL NAME
// is to hover over the field name in the List Settings page and look at the
URL.
oFldCtx.Templates.Fields = {"Order_x0020_Now":
{"View": overrideOrderNow} };

     // Register the template override
     SPClientTemplates.TemplateManager.RegisterTemplateOverrides(o-
FldCtx);

})();

function overrideOrderNow(ctx) {

     //Get the ID of the current row
     var nID = ctx.CurrentItem.ID;

     //
     //Build the String to display the button and launch the workflow...
     //
     // What is the relative URL of our site?
     var sSiteRelativeURL = "/sites/book1/shopcart";


     // sWorkflowURLPart1 is the workflow start page up to the unique list
item ID (look for "&ID=nnn" and copy up to but not including the nnn)
     var sWorkflowURLPart1 = sSiteRelativeURL + "/_layouts/15/IniWrkflIP.as-
px?List={9f9c865b-c87c-4068-a2a4-77cf40e1174f}&ID=";
```

```
    // sWorkflowURLPart2 is the remaining (after the ID) URL from the
workflow start page
    var  sWorkflowURLPart2  =  "&ItemGuid={C59467E2-AC14-4577-A5C1-
260CC34057E7}&TemplateID={079bf304-b8b4-42af-9439-fc3fbafed695}";

    // sButtonImage is the address of the button image to display
    var sButtonImage = sSiteRelativeURL + "/SiteAssets/order_now.png";

    // sReturnToPage is the URL of the page that the user will be returned to
after the Workflow launches
    var  sReturnToPage  =  sSiteRelativeURL  +  "/SitePages/Order%20Re-
ceived.aspx";

    //
    // Now Put it all together, in the format <a href='Workflow Start
URL'><img src='Button Image URL' /></a>
    var sOrderNowButtonHTML = "<a href='" + sWorkflowURLPart1 + nID +
sWorkflowURLPart2 + "&Source=" + sReturnToPage + "'> <img src='" + sBut-
tonImage + "' /></a>";

    //Return the Image tag as the new field value
    return sOrderNowButtonHTML;
}
```

Ideas for Enhancement

- Make the products list searchable rather than just using Group
  By views.

- Improve input forms by hiding fields that aren't relevant to the
  user during the ordering process and showing a different set
  of fields for a new order or a re-order (for example, by using
  content types or InfoPath forms.)

- Automatically alert the person who ordered when order status
  changes.

Governance Notes

- The Orders list can build up a large volume of content over
  time. Plan to regularly purge old orders so that the number of
  records in any view is less than 5,000.

- Consider who manages the *Products* and *Product Categories*
  lists and how.

All Staff Contact List

✧ See the Contact List **live and download the** printable Excel **at the** *SharePoint in Practice* **site (https://lightlever.sharepoint. com/sites/book1/Lists/contacts).**

Business Problem

How can we centrally manage all contact information, share it among all staff, and easily search, update, and access it through Outlook?

Practical Solution

The contact list is another out-of-the-box SharePoint feature that is sometimes underutilized. With a few customizations and some education, it can do a lot.

The most obvious use is the "one source of truth" place to keep names, phone numbers and email addresses for all the people you might need to contact. This could include internal (managers and colleagues) and external (vendor, travel agent, media contact, etc.). If you do have internal and external contacts in the contact list, use a choice field to flag each item as internal or external, and create views to serve up a staff-only version of the list.

SharePoint in Practice Design: Contact List

Contacts List

Web Address: */contacts*

SharePoint Description: *Stores contact information available to all staff and management for all internal and external contacts.*

This is a standard SharePoint contact list with some modifications as detailed below. The SharePoint contact list template provides *Connect to Outlook* capabilities as well as all standard SharePoint list features.

Metadata

Standard Contact columns, plus:

Metadata Field	Data Type	Manda-tory?	Default	Description
Contact Type	Choice • Staff • Consultant • Media • Vendor • Board Member • Volunteer	Yes	Staff	
Department	Choice • Accounting • Executive • Finance • HR • IT • Marketing • Operations	No	None	Could be a Site Column and/or a Look-up.
Staff Loca-tion	Choice • Central • Business • District • East Office • Head Office • Riverfront • South Shore • West Office	Yes	None	To which office is this contract primarily affil-iated? User can select only one (otherwise Group By views can't be used). Could create a site column and/or Look-up against a list.
Content Steward	Yes/No	Yes	No	Is this person named as a Content Steward?
Profile Picture	Person No groups. Dis-play as Picture only 48x48	No	None	A link to the SharePoint Profile for this user, used to display the picture of the person, and link to their user profile.

Views

- All Contact View
- Group by Branch: staff only, with photos (default view)
- Group by Type: all contacts, with photos
- Content Stewards

Ideas for Enhancement

- A useful trick with a contact list is to use it to generate an organization chart. This is done by adding a look-up field that (unintuitively) does a look-up on itself. In the contact list, create a look-up field *Reports To* that lists names in the same contact list. This will allow us to specify the "manager" for each contact and thus creates the staff-manager linkage needed to build an organization chart. The contact list—including the *Reports To* field, name, phone number, email address, job title, etc.—is exported to Excel, and we use the Microsoft Visio organization chart wizard to read the Excel spreadsheet as a data file. The organization chart will not update dynamically, but it can be updated periodically using this same process.

- Related to the above, you can use the Visio organization chart wizard to save an organization chart as a webpage. Visio produces an HTML file where you can search the org chart and click a person to view details.

- Consider how you use the *Contact Type* field—for example, management vs. staff vs. external, or employee vs. contractor. You can use views to display your contacts any way you need.

- If you are focused on internal contacts, you may include fields for *Role, Committee,* or *Location.* These can be used to create useful views to slice and dice the data. We often use this approach on large contact lists, and filter by "department" to display staff information on the department home page.

- Use an Excel spreadsheet that is linked to the contact list and is designed to be printed. (The contact list webpage does not print very well.) The contact list may be exported to Excel and formatted to be more print-friendly. Using the Export to Excel feature of SharePoint, you can easily keep this updated. See an **example** on the *SharePoint in Practice* site (**https://lightlever.sharepoint.com/sites/book1**).

- A different approach to the above is to create a stripped-down web-part page that is designed to be printed.

- Make a policy that this contact list the corporate "one source of truth," not just another place to search for contacts (in addition to Outlook, a printed directory, your HR system, etc.). To help it become that single source, and therefore more useful, consider including a business process where staff or managers keep this list up to date, and HR, IT, and others receive updates (Alerts) to trigger changes to their respective systems.

Governance Notes

- Decide who "owns" the contact data. Is each employee responsible to keep their own record up to date? Or is it HR's responsibility? Or individual department managers, Content Stewards, or Site Administrators?

- Include Version History on the contact list so you can see modification history, and undo any incorrect edits.

- If you generate an Org Chart from the contact list, decide who is responsible to update it, and when.

Document Management

❖ See the **Document Library** **live on the *SharePoint in Practice*** site (**https://lightlever.sharepoint.com/sites/book1/d**).

Business Problem

How can we manage documents, easily locate them, tag them for search, and ensure only the appropriate people can read or edit?

Practical Solution

Document management is a big topic, but much can be done using SharePoint document libraries "out-of-the-box." In its most basic form, our document management system is a document library with version history, some added metadata, and views to support efficient use.

Ensure you understand SharePoint *Site Columns* and *Content Types* when designing and implementing document management solutions.

When focusing on document management, we modify our default views to include the *Version* and the *Check-in Comments* fields. Comments are updated when someone checks in a document and is normally only displayed in version history.

Including a document status field is helpful. This may be a simple flag to indicate *Draft* or *Final*, or more complex, such as *initial, under development, under review,* or *final*. Build views in the document library that group documents by Status. This view may exclude draft versions and make it easier for people to find the documents they are working on.

Another useful SharePoint feature that is sometimes overlooked is *major and minor version history*. The default versioning setting in SharePoint Online document libraries is *major versions* only. Adding minor (also known as *draft*) versions gives more control, as well as more responsibility. Examples requiring major and minor versions include large documents maintained by a group of people and published on occasion, such as an employee handbook or a policies and procedures manual.

Minor (draft) versions allow editors to modify documents as they wish, while delaying publishing of changes to the general populous until fully ready. In the screen shot below you will see you have the choice of setting who can see draft versions. One option is only *editors* (people who can edit the file), and that is usually best.

In document management, remember the power of *SharePoint Alerts*. Having the built-in ability to set and manage alerts is powerful: users informed and can easily see *what* has been changed and *when*. Alerts can be set on the entire document library or for specific folders or individual files. Generally, Alerts are managed by the "alertee"—the user receiving the alert—but a Site Administrator can create an alert for any user.

Your document library may include a *Review Date* or *Archive Date* metadata field. This field indicates when a file will be archived. Set a default of, for example, [TODAY]+730 (two years). An "Ready to Archive" view can be driven from this field, or a SharePoint Workflow may wait for this date to pass and then move the file to an archive library and/or delete it.

Be careful about making metadata mandatory. If mandatory, users must take the time to fill fields when adding files to a library. This ensures they are paying attention to that (all-important) metadata but can cause issues when bulk uploading. When files are added to a document library using drag-and-drop, the presence of mandatory metadata will cause the files to remain checked out until all mandatory fields are filled. The files must be checked in one by one. This can be labor intensive.

Generally, only make metadata mandatory when absolutely necessary to drive specific views or searches.

Finally, define (in the Governance Guide) standards for file and folder naming to support consistency and ease of finding files. Generally, it is best to include spaces or dashes (or in some SharePoint versions, underscores) as word separators in your file names. With these separators the SharePoint search crawler can identify and index individual words to make them findable. For example, a file named "CorporateBudget.xlsx" will not be findable when searching for "corporate" or "budget" unless those tags appear elsewhere in the metadata or in the file contents. Naming this file "Corporate-Budget.xlsx" allows search to index the separate words and can improve search results and user experience.

SharePoint in Practice Design: Document Management Library

Document Management Library

Web Address: */d*

SharePoint Description: *Example document library for document management.*

Content Types

The following content types are available in this library:

- *SIP[8] Document* – the standard Document content type, with metadata fields attached.

- *SIP Link to Document* – the standard Link to Document content type, with metadata fields attached.

---

8   Here SIP is our short name of *SharePoint in Practice*. Content Types should have clear names.

Metadata

The following metadata fields are used in this library.

Metadata Field	Data Type	Manda-tory?	Default	Description
Business Area	Site Column: Department or Division	Yes	None	Which part of the business "owns" this document
Document Type	Site Column: Document Type	Yes	None	What is the classification of this document?
Archive Date	Date	No	[TODAY] +730	When should this document be archived or deleted?
Status	Choice: • 1-Draft • 2-In Progress • 3-Under Review • 4-Final • 5-Archived	Yes	Draft	

Views

The following Views will be used in this library:

1. *All Documents* – default view with all metadata shown, in folders

2. *Recent* – all documents shown without folders, sorted descending by modified date

3. *Group by Business Area*

4. *Group by Editor* – grouping by *Modified*, who last modified the Document

5. *Final Documents* – filter to exclude any files not tagged as 4-Final

Ideas for Enhancement

- Consider implementing a records management system. There are many available that integrate with SharePoint, or you might use Managed Metadata to set up and apply your own hierarchy of tags.

- Add workflows and views to implement an auto-archive capability.

- Using managed metadata, use "Column Default Value Settings" to set default metadata based on folders.

- Consider adding metadata fields as search refiners on your default search page.

- Consider using managed metadata navigation and filtering (**https://tinyurl.com/ManagedMetadata**) for a rich search and filter experience alongside the document library.

Governance Notes

- If you are relying on metadata to be entered for views and search refiners, create a policy that certain fields are required, make them mandatory, and educate user on *why* and *how* to use mandatory metadata.

- Set a policy (in your Governance Guide) to limit unique permissions to the *folder level* and not individual documents. Setting permissions granularity any finer than *folder* creates a challenging permission management scenario. If unique permissions are required, create a folder and apply the permissions there, at the folder level. Files saved in that folder inherit the unique permissions. Then, regardless of which view (including non-folder views) is used, permission trimming works nicely.

- Train and support the widespread use of SharePoint version history. Unless required for some business process, train people to not use "Save As..." to rename documents, adding their initials, edited dates, and the like. With version history, we can easily see *who made what edits when*, and can use Word to compare two document versions.

Permissions Tracker

❖ **See the Permissions Tracker live on the *SharePoint in Practice* site (https://lightlever.sharepoint.com/sites/book1/Lists/ permissions).**

Business Problem

How can we efficiently track who manages SharePoint permissions for the various objects in your site?

Practical Solution

SharePoint permissions can get messy, especially in a complex site managed by a team. This permission tracker is one way to track and quickly view who is managing the various objects and *who can do what to what*. In this custom list, each object links to its relevant permission groups. The downside of this list is that it must be maintained. Note that the Portal Design Document template described in Part 1 includes a Word-based version of this tracker.

SharePoint in Practice: Permissions Tracker

Permissions Tracker List

Web Address: */permissions*

SharePoint Description: *This list tracks "who can do what" in the portal.*

This is a custom SharePoint list as detailed below. Note the links to User Groups can be useful shortcuts, and because not everyone has access to Site Settings screens to navigate to view group listings. For this list, Version History and Content Approval are both enabled to better manage change. Permissions on this list itself are set so anyone can read but only SharePoint Site Administrators can edit.

Metadata

This custom list is structured as follows.

Metadata Field	Data Type	Mandatory?	Default	Description
Object Name	Single line of text	Mandatory	None	The name of the SharePoint object (rename the standard Title field)
Object URL	Hyperlink	Mandatory	None	The address of the object for clarity and ease of access
Department	Site column	Optional	None	Which Department or Division does this object fall under?
Primary Administrator	Person field	Mandatory	None	Who is the primary administrator for this Object? Displayed with picture and presence. May be selectable from SharePoint Administrators group.
Backup Administrators	Person field Allow multiple	Optional	None	Who is/are the secondary administrator(s) for this project?
Inherited?	Choice • Inherited • Unique	Mandatory	Inherited	Does this object inherit permissions from its parent?
Inherited from Object	Look-up on this same list "Object Name"	Optional	None	If Unique permissions, this is blank; if Inherited, this lists the parent *Object Name*.
Unique Permissions Groups	Person or Group Allow multiple Groups	Optional		For Unique permissions objects, list the SharePoint groups who have permissions. Configure so the link is clickable to view the user group members.
Unique Approved By	Person	Optional		For Unique permissions objects, tracks **Who** approved the unique permissions (SharePoint User name)
Unique Approved Date	Date and Time	Optional	None	For Unique permissions objects, tracks **When** the above "who" approved the unique permissions

Metada-ta Field	Data Type	Manda-tory?	De-fault	Description
Comments		Optional		Any comments relating to this item

Views

- All items view
- My Objects: showing objects where the current user is the primary or backup admin ([Primary Administrator]=[Me] OR [Backup Administrators] contains [Me])
- Group by Administrator
- Group by Department

Ideas for Enhancement

- If a user does not have permission to view or modify membership on a permission group, the group links will not work for them. Configure permissions groups to allow everyone to see group membership.

- Install a workflow that changes the permissions in the named object automatically when you change the Permissions Tracker list.

- Include additional fields to track permissions levels (read, contribute, edit, full control, etc.) for each object and group, rather than just listing groups.

- Consider how the links to groups work with Office 365 groups. (Current example only tested with SharePoint groups.)

Governance Notes

- Ensure alerts are set for Site Administrators to immediately know the permissions tracker is being updated.

- Set unique permissions on this list such that only the appropriate group of users (e.g., Content Stewards and/or Site Administrators) has rights to change this list.

- The permissions tracker list is an example of a list that becomes useless and even misleading if not maintained, so be fastidious. Review at your Content Stewards meetings. Be sure everyone—especially Site Administrators and Content Stewards—are aware of the Permissions Tracker and their responsibility to keep it up-to-date. This list is very useful if it contains accurate information.

APPENDICES

Links to *SharePoint in Practice* Online Resources

The following table provides a summary of the links in the body of this book. These are repeated here for convenience. As the *SharePoint in Practice* body of work continues to grow and improve, be sure to check our Office 365 Companion site (**https://lightlever.sharepoint.com/sites/book1**) for recent updates.

Template Name and Link	Format	Chapter	Notes
Board Portal	Working list and library in SharePoint Online	Part 2	See Part 2 for details
Communication Plan	Word	Chapter 6	
Contact List	Printable Excel spreadsheet	Part 2	See Part 2 for details
Contact List	Working list in SharePoint Online	Part 2	See Part 2 for details

Template Name and Link	Format	Chapter	Notes
Content Migration Checklist	Word	Chapter 7	
Content Migration Plan	Word	Chapter 7	
Content Stewards Meeting Agenda	Word	Chapter 8	
Content Stewards Terms of Reference	Word	Chapter 8	
Content Stewards Training 1	PowerPoint	Chapter 9	
Content Stewards Training 2	PowerPoint	Chapter 9	
Design Team Kick-off Presentation	PowerPoint	Chapter 3	
Design Team Terms of Reference	Word	Chapter 3	
Document Library	Working library in SharePoint Online	Part 2	See Part 2 for details
Executive Overview Presentation	PowerPoint	Chapter 6, Chapter 9	
File Naming Conventions	Word	Chapter 3, Chapter 7, Chapter 8	
Go-Live Contest and Training Survey	Word	Chapter 2, Chapter 6	
Go-Live Plan	Word	Chapter 2	An hour-long webcast to introduce the new system to all staff.
Go-Live Webinar	PowerPoint	Chapter 9	
Governance Committee Terms of Reference	Word	Chapter 8	
Governance Guide	Word	Chapter 8	

Template Name and Link	Format	Chapter	Notes
Leave Calendar	Working list in SharePoint Online	Part 2	See Part 2 for details
Migration Team Kick-off Presentation	PowerPoint	Chapter 7	
Order Now button	Image	Part 2	See Part 2 for details
Permissions Tracker	Working list in SharePoint Online	Part 2	See Part 2 for details
Pilot Participants Kick-off Presentation	PowerPoint	Chapter 5	
Pilot Plan	Word	Chapter 5	
Policy Manual	Working wiki in SharePoint Online	Part 2	See Part 2 for details
Portal Design Document	Word	Chapter 3	The core document for designing the system. Used extensively throughout the project.
Portal Design Graphics	Visio	Chapter 3	
Portal Development Project Plan	Word	Chapter 2	
Project Change Request	Word	Chapter 2	
Project Charter	Word	Chapter 2	
Project Status Report	Word	Chapter 2	
Quick Reference Sheet	Word	Chapter 9	
Sign-Off Sheet	Word	Chapter 2 and 4	
Shopping Cart	Working list in SharePoint Online	Part 2	See Part 2 for details

Template Name and Link	Format	Chapter	Notes
Shopping Cart JavaScript	JavaScript file	Part 2	See Part 2 for details
Steering Committee Kick-off Presentation	PowerPoint	Chapter 2	
Steering Committee Terms of Reference	Word	Chapter 2	
SharePoint Administrator Training	PowerPoint	Chapter 9	
Suggestion Box	Working list in SharePoint Online	Part 2	See Part 2 for details
"The Shopping Cart Story"	PowerPoint	Part 2	See Part 2 for details
Timesheet	Working list in SharePoint Online	Part 2	See Part 2 for details
Timesheet Report	Excel spreadsheet	Part 2	See Part 2 for details

APPENDIX B

Other Useful Links

Lightlever blog: **https://lightlever.ca/blog**

Lightlever YouTube channel: **https://www.youtube.com/user/ gerrybrim**

Gerry Brimacombe Twitter: **https://twitter.com/gbrim**

Gerry Brimacombe Facebook: **https://www.facebook.com/ gerrybrim**

Gerry Brimacombe LinkedIn: **https://www.linkedin.com/in/ gerrybrimacombe**

SharePoint in Practice list templates: **https://sharepointinpractice. com/resources/**

Microsoft Office 365 Training Centre **https://support.office.com/ office-training-center**

Video: Contrasting wikis and document libraries: **https://www.youtube.com/watch?v=n84kRMDLV8Q**

Video: Convert document to SharePoint wiki: **https://www.youtube.com/watch?v=XlM8TJvTql4**

SherWeb Canadian and US web hosting: **https://www.sherweb.com/sharepoint/?aid=15319**

SharePoint Fest SharePoint conferences: **https://sharepointfest.com**

European SharePoint, Office 365, & Azure Conference **http://www.sharepointeurope.com**

Microsoft Office 365 Canadian product comparison site: **https://products.office.com/en-ca/compare-all-microsoft-office-products?tab=2**

Glossary

Term / Abbreviation	Meaning
Content Migration	The process of moving files and other materials from "wherever they are" to the portal.
Content Steward	A SharePoint "power user" who supports the people in their business area.
Design Document	The core document to the *SharePoint in Practice* method—developed during the design phase and used and updated throughout the project. Repurposed for governance, and training.
DNS	Domain Name Service – internet address book
Go-Live	The transition from development to day-to-day use of the portal.
Governance Committee	A group of people governing the management and changes to the portal.
Intranet	A website that uses Internet protocols and technology, but is limited to users internal to a company, team or group. In this book, for simplicity we are using *intranet* and *portal* synonymously.
Migration Team	The team responsible for migrating content to the intranet.

Term / Abbreviation	Meaning
MS	Microsoft
OOTB	See Out-of-the-box
Out-of-the-box	Standard SharePoint tools as installed, without serious, specialized programming. Out-of-the-box tools are fundamentally the SharePoint web interface and SharePoint designer.
Portal (or Company Portal)	An intranet that is customized to support staff collaboration and access to information. In this book, for simplicity we are using *intranet* and *portal* synonymously.
PM	Project Manager
scope creep	In a project, when small, undocumented or unmanaged changes are gradually added to what is to be accomplished. Sometimes called "death by a thousand cuts"
site structure diagram	An image depicting the hierarchical structure of a SharePoint site..
Support Video	A short "how to video" demonstrating some specific feature of the portal.
Webinar	A style of training, largely one-directional, delivered over the web, for example with Skype for Business or GoToMeeting.

About the Author

Gerry Brimacombe is a SharePoint consultant and trainer whose unquenchable thirst for better/faster/easier ways of doing everything has led him to produce methods and templates to engage business users and create no-code SharePoint sites.

Gerry has been studying technology since 1981 and studying people much longer. He has a degree in Computer Science and a Graduate Certificate in Project Management. Gerry's knowledge of SharePoint feeds his passion to build or improve intranet solutions that save his clients money and allow them to work effectively from anywhere, every day.

The methods and templates in this book are gleaned from Gerry's experience working with many clients developing and supporting their SharePoint solutions. Contact him through **lightlever.ca** to help with your SharePoint projects, including business analysis, project management, development, consulting, training, or speaking engagements.

Gerry welcomes your questions and constructive feedback on *SharePoint in Practice,* his first book. Please email him at **gerry@lightlever.ca**.

Index

Printed in Great Britain
by Amazon

77447927R00102